THE ENTERTAINER

by the same author

LOOK BACK IN ANGER

THE ENTERTAINER

EPITAPH FOR GEORGE DILLON
(with Anthony Creighton)

THE WORLD OF PAUL SLICKEY

A SUBJECT OF SCANDAL AND CONCERN
A play for television

LUTHER

PLAYS FOR ENGLAND
The Blood of the Bambergs and *Under Plain Cover*

UNDER PLAIN COVER

INADMISSIBLE EVIDENCE

A PATRIOT FOR ME

A BOND HONOURED

TIME PRESENT and THE HOTEL IN AMSTERDAM

TOM JONES
A film script

THE RIGHT PROSPECTUS
A play for television

VERY LIKE A WHALE
A play for television

WEST OF SUEZ

HEDDA GABLER
(adapted from Henrik Ibsen)

THE GIFT OF FRIENDSHIP
A play for television

A SENSE OF DETACHMENT

A PLACE CALLING ITSELF ROME

THE PICTURE OF DORIAN GRAY
(adapted from Oscar Wilde)

THE
ENTERTAINER

JOHN OSBORNE

ff

faber and faber

LONDON · BOSTON

First published in 1957
by Faber and Faber Limited
3 Queen Square London WC1N 3AU
First published in this edition 1961
Reprinted 1965, 1967, 1969, 1972, 1974, 1983,
1986 and 1987
Printed in Great Britain by
Cox & Wyman Ltd., Reading
All rights reserved

All professional inquiries in regard to this play
should be addressed to the author's agent, Margery
Vosper Ltd., 53a Shaftesbury Avenue, London, W.1,
and all amateur inquiries should be addressed to
Messrs. Evans Brothers Ltd., Montague House,
Russell Square, London, WC1

ISBN 0 571 06367 5 (Faber Paper Covered Editions)
ISBN 0 571 07050 7 (hard bound edition)

To A.C.

who remembers what it was like, and will not
forget it; who, I hope, will never let me forget
it—not while there is still a Paradise Street and
Claypit Lane to go back to

NOTE

The music hall is dying, and, with it, a significant part of England. Some of the heart of England has gone; something that once belonged to everyone, for this was truly a folk art. In writing this play, I have not used some of the techniques of the music hall in order to exploit an effective trick, but because I believe that these can solve some of the eternal problems of time and space that face the dramatist, and, also, it has been relevant to the story and setting. Not only has this technique its own traditions, its own convention and symbol, its own mystique, it cuts right across the restrictions of the so-called naturalistic stage. Its contact is immediate, vital, and direct.

CAST

BILLY RICE

JEAN RICE

ARCHIE RICE

PHOEBE RICE

FRANK RICE

WILLIAM (BROTHER BILL) RICE

GRAHAM DODD

CONTENTS

OVERTURE

1. Billy and Jean.
2. Archie Rice—"Don't Take Him Seriously!"
3. Billy, Jean and Phoebe.
4. Archie Rice—"In Trouble Again".
5. Billy, Jean, Phoebe and Archie.

INTERMISSION

6. Billy, Phoebe, Jean, Archie and Frank.
7. Archie Rice—"Interrupts the Programme."
8. Billy, Phoebe, Jean, Archie and Frank.

INTERMISSION

9. Frank Rice—Singing For You.
10. Billy, Phoebe, Jean, Archie and Frank.
11. The Good Old Days Again.
12. Jean and Graham—Archie and Bill.
13. Archie Rice—The One and Only.

The first performance in Great Britain of THE ENTERTAINER was given at the Royal Court Theatre, Sloane Square, London, on 10th April 1957 by the English Stage Company. It was directed by Tony Richardson and the decor was by Alan Tagg. The cast was as follows:

BILLY RICE	George Relph
JEAN RICE	Dorothy Tutin
PHOEBE RICE	Brenda de Banzie
ARCHIE RICE	Laurence Olivier
FRANK RICE	Richard Pasco
GORGEOUS GLADYS	Vivienne Drummond
WILLIAM (BROTHER BILL) RICE	Aubrey Dexter
GRAHAM	Stanley Meadows

SETTING: The action takes place in a large coastal
resort. The house where the Rice family live is one of
those tall ugly monuments built by a prosperous
business man at the beginning of the century. Only
twenty-five minutes in the brougham to the front. Now,
trolley buses hum past the front drive, full of workers
from the small factories that have grown up round
about. This is a part of the town the holiday makers
never see—or, if they do, they decide to turn back to
the pleasure gardens. This is what they have spent two
or three hours in a train to escape. They don't even
have to pass it on their way in from the central station,
for this is a town on its own, and it has its own station,
quite a large one, with acres of goods sheds and shunt-
ing yards. However, the main line trains don't stop
there. It is not residential, it is hardly industrial. It is
full of dirty blank spaces, high black walls, a gas
holder, a tall chimney, a main road that shakes with
dust and lorries. The shops are scattered at the corners
of narrow streets. A newsagent's, a general grocer's, a
fish-and-chip shop.

OVERTURE

During the Intermissions, an advertising sheet
is lowered.

NUMBER ONE

At the back a gauze. Behind it, a part of the town. In
front of it, a high rostrum with steps leading to it.
Knee-high flats and a door frame will serve for a wall.
The sight-lines are preserved by swagging. Different
swags can be lowered for various scenes to break up
the acting areas. Also, ordinary, tatty backcloth and

draw-tabs. There are two doors L. and R. of the apron. The lighting is the kind you expect to see in the local Empire—everything bang-on, bright and hard, or a simple follow-spot. The scenes and interludes must, in fact, be lit as if they were simply turns on the bill. Furniture and props are as basic as they would be for a short sketch. On both sides of the proscenium is a square in which numbers—the turn numbers—appear. The problems involved are basically the same as those that confront any resident stage-manager on the twice nightly circuit every Monday morning of his working-life.

Music. The latest, the loudest, the worst. A gauzed front-cloth. On it are painted enormous naked young ladies, waving brightly coloured fans, and kicking out gaily. Written across it in large letters are the words "ROCK'N ROLL NEW'D LOOK".

Behind the up-stage gauze, light picks out an old man. He walks across the stage from L. to R. As he reaches C. he pauses and looks up. There are shouts and screams. The noise of a woman trying to separate two men—her son and her lover perhaps. Cries of "Oh leave him alone! Don't! Please don't! Leave him *alone*". He walks off R. and reappears beside the swagging, walking in C. There is a crash and the sounds of blows. He pauses again, then goes on. The woman screams, loudly this time. He pauses again, turns back, and shouts down over the banister rail "Do you mind being quiet down there, please." He pauses, but there is no response. "*Will you* kindly stop making all that noise!" He manages to sound dignified, but he has a powerful voice and the noise stops for a moment. He nods and starts moving. A voice shouts "Why don't you shut your great big old gob, you poor, bloody old fool!" A woman's sob stabs the end of the sentence and the old man hesitates, turns back and calls over the stairs "Are you all right, Mrs. ——?" A man's voice is heard, urgent and heated. A door bangs, and the noise is muffled. The sobbing is still audible but the situation seems to be more controlled. The old man returns C. and enters through the door-frame.

BILLY RICE is a spruce man in his seventies. He has great physical pride, the result of a life-time of being admired as a "fine figure of a man". He is slim, upright, athletic. He glows with scrubbed well-being. His hair is just grey, thick and silky from its vigorous daily brush. His clothes are probably twenty-five years old—including his pointed patent leather shoes—but well-pressed and smart. His watch chain gleams, his collar is fixed with a tie-pin beneath the tightly knotted black tie, his brown homburg is worn at a very slight angle. When he speaks it is with a dignified Edwardian diction —a kind of repudiation of both Oxford and cockney that still rhymes "cross" with "force", and yet manages to avoid being exactly upper-class or effete. Indeed, it is not an accent of class but of period. One does not hear it often now.

Take up front gauze.

He walks down C, laying down a folded newspaper, two quart bottles of beer, and a telegram, which he glances at quickly. He crosses to the fore-stage door R., and goes through it singing sonorously but cheerfully:

>   "Rock of Ages cleft for me
>   Let me hide myself in thee!"

He reappears in his shirt sleeves pulling on a heavy woollen cardigan over his waistcoat. Still singing, he sits down, pours himself out a glass of beer, and starts to unlace his shoes. He puts these in a box with tissue paper up-stage C. The noise starts up again from downstairs. He drinks from his glass of beer, takes out a nail file and stands cleaning his nails expertly. This is like flicking off the old, imaginary speck of dust. There is a yell from downstairs. BILLY speaks, gravely, with forethought.

BILLY: Bloody Poles and Irish!

He sits down and puts on his carpet slippers. Front door

slams, he takes spectacles from his case and puts them on.
I hate the bastards.

*He unfolds his newspaper, the doorbell is still ringing. He
looks irritated, but he has his feet up and is too com-
fortable to move. He sings cheerfully, as if to drown the
noise of the doorbell.*

BILLY: Nearer my God to Thee

Nearer to Thee!

He listens and then goes on.

Even though it be a cross

That raiseth me

He picks up the newspaper and peers at it gravely.

Still all my song would be

Nearer my God to Thee,

Nearer to Thee!

He puts down his paper.

(*Standing*). Why don't they answer the bloody door!

*He leans his arms on the chair, wondering whether he will
have to go after all.*

Ought to be locked up, some of these people.

*It looks as though he won't have to go after all, and he
settles back cheerfully,*

Dirty, filthy lot. (*Picks up paper. Pushes paper down
suddenly.*)

My God, there's a draught!

Gets up and goes to door and looks out.

I'll bet they've left the front door open. Born in fields,
they are.

Takes a rug and arranges it against the door.

Probably were born in fields. Animals. (*Back to chair
and sits down*). Like animals. Wild animals.

*He settles down. Across from up L. comes a young girl.
Billy pours himself out some more beer. The girl knocks on
the door. He listens.*

Who is it?

The girl knocks again.

Who is it? Can't get any peace in this damned house.

GIRL: Is that you, Grandad?

BILLY: What?

GIRL: It's Jean.

BILLY: (*rising*). Who is it?

JEAN: It's me—Jean.

BILLY: (*goes to door and stands behind it*). Can't even read the paper in peace. Who?

JEAN: It's your granddaughter.

Jean tries to push the door open but the rug prevents it.

BILLY: Just a minute! Just a minute! Hold your horses! (*He bends down*).

JEAN: Sorry.

BILLY: Hold your horses!

He releases the rug and opens the door, revealing Jean Rice. She is about twenty-two, dark, with slightly protruding teeth and bad eyesight. She is what most people would call plain, but already humour and tenderness have begun to stake their small claims around her nose and eyes. Her mouth is large, generous.

JEAN: Hello, Grandad.

BILLY: I wondered who the hell it was.

JEAN: I'm sorry.

BILLY: I thought it was some of that mad lot carrying on. Well, come in if you're coming, it's draughty standing about in the doorway. I've only just sat down.

JEAN: (*coming in*). Did I disturb you, I am sorry.

BILLY: I'd just sat down to read the evening paper. It's a bloody farm-yard this place.

JEAN: Well, how are you?

BILLY: Bloody farm-yard. They want locking up. And you know what now, don't you? You know who she's got upstairs, in Mick's old room, don't you? Some black fellow. It's true. I tell you, you've come to a mad-house this time.

JEAN: You're looking very well. How do you feel?

BILLY: I'm all right. You expect a few aches and pains when you get to my age. Phoebe's at the pictures, I think. She didn't tell me you were coming.

JEAN: I didn't tell her.

BILLY: No, well she didn't say anything. So I wasn't expecting a knock on the door.

JEAN: I only decided to come up this morning.

BILLY: I'd only just sat down to read the evening paper.

JEAN: I'm sorry. I disturbed you.

She has picked up her cue neatly. The fact that his evening has been disturbed is established. His air of distracted irritation relaxes and he smiles a little. He is pleased to see her anyway.

BILLY: Well, give your Grandad a kiss, come on.

She does so.

JEAN: It's good to see you.

BILLY: Well, it's nice to see you, my darling. Bit of a surprise. Go on, take your things off.

Jean undoes her coat, and throws a packet of cigarettes on the table.

JEAN: Got you those.

BILLY: Phoebe won't be long. What she went out for, I don't know.

JEAN: Gone to the pictures has she?

BILLY: She's mad. Oh, that's very kind of you. Very kind. Thank you. Yes, she said she was going early. I don't know why she can't stay in.

JEAN: Well, you know—she's always been like that. She enjoys it.

BILLY: Well, she'll have to learn. She's not a youngster any more. When she gets to my age, she won't want to do it.

He unwraps the cigarettes and takes out an ivory holder from his waistcoat.

Oh, this is nice of you. Thank you. Still, if she stays in she only gets irritable. And I can't stand rows. Not any more. (*He stares in front of him*). No use arguing with Phoebe anyway. Would you like some beer?

She shakes her head.

She just won't listen to you. Are you sure you won't? There's a damn great crate out in the kitchen, Frank brought it in this morning.

16

JEAN: No thanks, Grandad.

BILLY: No, when she gets in that mood, I just go out.

JEAN: Where do you go?

BILLY: I go for a walk. Or I go to the Club. You haven't been to the Club. Oh, I must take you then. It's very quiet, mind you. Except at week-ends. You get some of the wives then. But they're mostly oldtimers like me.

JEAN: Sounds fun.

BILLY: Well, it's somewhere to go when you're fed up with the place. Don't suppose it would appeal much to youngsters like yourself. I expect you go in more for these jazz places.

JEAN: I'd like to go. You must take me.

BILLY: Would you really? Would you? All right. But, I warn you, there's none of your boogie-woogie. How long are you here for?

JEAN: Just the week-end.

BILLY: We'll go tomorrow night. It's a good night, Sunday. I sing them some of the old songs, sometimes, when I feel like it. Haven't done it lately, not for a long time. Don't seem to feel like it.

JEAN: Where's Dad?

BILLY: He's at the theatre. He's playing here—at the Grand this week, you know.

JEAN: Oh, yes, of course.

BILLY: I don't seem to feel like it these days. You get a bit depressed sometimes sitting here. Oh, then there's the Cambridge down the road. I go there, of course. But there's not the old crowd there, you know. What about the news, eh? That's depressing. What d'you make of all this business out in the Middle East? People seem to be able to do what they like to us. Just what they like. I don't understand it. I really don't. Archie goes to that damned place down by the clock tower.

JEAN: The Rockliffe.

BILLY: Yes, the Rockliffe. Every tart and pansy boy in the district are in that place at a week-end. Archie tried to

17

get me there the other day. No thank you. It's just a meat-market.

JEAN: How is Dad?

BILLY: He's a fool.

JEAN: Oh?

BILLY: Putting money into a road-show.

JEAN: I didn't know.

BILLY: Oh, it's another of his cock-eyed ideas. He won't listen to me. He spends half his time in that Rockliffe.

JEAN: I see. What show is it this time?

BILLY: Oh, I don't remember what it's called.

JEAN: Have you seen it?

BILLY: No, I haven't seen it. I wouldn't. These nudes. They're killing the business. Anyway, I keep telling him—it's dead already. Has been for years. It was all over, finished, dead when I got out of it. I saw it coming. I saw it coming, and I got out. They don't want real people any more.

JEAN: No, I suppose they don't.

BILLY: They don't want human-beings. Not any more. Wish he wouldn't get stuck in that Rockliffe. Gets half his posing girls in there if you ask me. (*Warming up.*) Well, why should a family man take his wife and kids to see a lot of third-class sluts standing about in the nude? It's not even as if they got the figures nowadays. They're all skin and bone.

JEAN: (*smiles*). Like me.

BILLY: Well, you don't stand around with nothing on for everyone to gaup at and God bless you for it. But you never see a woman with a really good figure now. I could tell you something about beautiful women now, I could. And it wasn't all make-up either. They were ladies. Ladies, and you took off your hat before you dared speak to them. Now! why, half the time you can't tell the women from the men. Not from the back. And even at the front you have to take a good look, sometimes.

JEAN: Like the Government and the Opposition.

18

BILLY: What's that? Like the Government and the Opposition. Don't talk to me about the Government. Or that other lot. Grubby lot of rogues. Want locking up. No, old Archie's a fool. He won't even listen to you. That's why I put up with old Phoebe. She's had to cope I can tell you. But I don't have to tell you. He's going to come a cropper I'm afraid. And pretty soon too. He's bitten off more than he can chew.

JEAN: With this new show you mean. Has he really put money into it?

BILLY: Put money into it! Don't make me laugh! He hasn't got two halfpennies for a penny. It's all credit. Credit, if you please! How he gets it beats me, after that last business. Still, he could always talk, your Dad. And that's about all. Do you know, I spent thousands of pounds on his education. Went to the same school as me. And his brother. Thousands of pounds. He wasn't one of these scholarship people, like you. And where's it got 'em? (*He takes a drink.*) That Rockliffe. They should close the place. Someone should write to the Council about it. I'm surprised nobody hasn't. There's a lot of gentry here, you know—Besides the riff-raff round here. Retired people. They don't want that kind of thing going on. Are you all right? You look as though you've been keeping late nights or something. What have you been doing with yourself? Lots of these parties, eh?

JEAN: No, not really.

BILLY: Well, you've got to have a good time while you're young. You won't get it later on. I'll bet he won't be in till all hours tonight.

JEAN: Dad?

BILLY: I'm very pleased to see you, Jean. Are you all right? They're treating you right?

JEAN: Oh, yes.

BILLY: They're doing right by you, I hope. You're not in any trouble, are you?

JEAN: No, Grandad. I'm not in any trouble.

19

BILLY: I just wondered why you came up to see us like this suddenly.

JEAN: Oh, it's just——

BILLY: I'm not asking you to tell me. You do as you like, my darling. I 'spect you're hungry are you?

JEAN: I ate on the train.

BILLY: You shouldn't have done that. It's extravagant, and all they give you is a lot of rubbish. You're not extravagant, are you?

JEAN: I don't think so.

BILLY: No, I didn't think so. You're a good girl, Jean. You'll get somewhere. I know you'll get somewhere. You're not like the lot in this house. You'll do something for yourself. You take after your old grandfather.

She smiles at him affectionately.

Don't you? Jean, if ever you're in any kind of trouble, you will come to me now won't you?

JEAN: I will.

BILLY: I mean it. Now look—there's just the two of us here. Promise me you'll come and tell me.

JEAN: Of course I will, but there's nothing——

BILLY: I'm not fooling about, I'm serious. Phoebe will be back any minute, and I don't want her to know. I want you to promise me.

JEAN: I promise you. If there is anything——

BILLY: If it's money, mind——

JEAN: Well I tell you I've just——

BILLY: I've got a few pounds in the Post Office. Not much, mind you, but I've got a few pounds. Nobody knows, so not to say a word, mind.

JEAN: No.

BILLY: Not even the pension people. I don't tell them my business. But, as I say——

JEAN: Grandad, I promise. If I want anything——

BILLY: Probably don't give you much in that job, do they? You tell 'em what you're worth, they're robbers.

JEAN: They pay pretty well.

20

BILLY: How much was your fare up here? (*He is getting slightly carried away*.)

JEAN: No, Grandad, please—I don't want it.

BILLY: Hold your bloody noise. If I want to give it to you, you shall have it. Here just a minute——

JEAN: Please——

BILLY: What's the matter? Isn't it good enough for you?

JEAN: It isn't that——

BILLY: Well then. Do as you're told and take it. I wouldn't have dared argue with my grandfather. Even at your age. (*Counting out his money*.) Um. Well, I don't seem to have enough just now. How much is it?

JEAN: I don't remember.

BILLY: Of course you remember. Look, there's half a quid. You take that towards it for now, and on Monday I'll go to the Post Office and get it out for you.

JEAN: Darling, you'll need that for the week-end. There's cigarettes and papers, and you're taking me to the Club, remember?

BILLY: Oh. Yes. I'd forgotten that. Well, we'll call it a loan, mind?

JEAN: A loan?

BILLY: Yes, a loan. You know what a loan is.

JEAN: Oh, all right.

BILLY: You mustn't go short. We all need looking after. And you've got to look after your own kind. No use leaving it to the Government for them to hand out to a lot of bleeders who haven't got the gumption to do anything for themselves. I want to look after you, Jean. I do, I do really. You're a good girl and I know you'll do something with your life, you'll *be* somebody. You won't waste it away and be silly.

JEAN: Bless you.

BILLY: Don't waste it. Do something good with it. Don't waste it. Sit down, for God's sake. You look as if you're going to put on your hat and coat and go. Sit down and talk to your Grandad. I don't get much chance to talk to anyone. They think you're a bit soft. Just because you can remember things when they were a bit different. Go on, have a glass.

JEAN: Thank you.

BILLY: Like that barmaid in the Cambridge. I don't go there so much. I've seen her laughing up her sleeve. She thinks I haven't seen her, but I am not soft. She's a common bit of goods, too. Great bosoms sticking out here. As if you want to see that, when you lean over for your drink. Enough to put you off your beer. And she gives short measure. You've got to watch them. They think they can have it over you.

JEAN: What time does the second house finish?

BILLY: I don't know. About eleven I suppose. You'll wait up all night if you wait for him. They wouldn't have employed someone like that in the old days. Like a common prostitute.

JEAN: Perhaps I should go and meet him.

BILLY: Do as you like, my girl. But I shouldn't. They've got a television in that bar now. A television. Now who do you think would want a television in a pub? Blaring away, you can't hear yourself think. D'you know? Do you know I asked them to turn it down, the other night. That cow with the bosom. Well, you'd expect her to be insolent. But then I asked the Gov'nor— Charlie Rowse. He's a pal of mine. I've known him for years. And do you know—he wouldn't hear of it! I don't know what's happening to everyone. I don't. Do you know?

JEAN: (*she isn't listening*). No, Grandad I don't.

BILLY: It makes you sad—sometimes. Old Charlie Rowse of all people. I haven't been able to go in there since, somehow. I got these in the off-licence over the way. (*He looks at her shrewdly.*) I suppose you've no right to expect people to listen to you. Just because you've had your life. It's all over for you. Why should anyone listen to you? (*Pause.*) Have you been drinking?

JEAN: Yes.

BILLY: I always know when a woman's been drinking.

JEAN: I'm sorry.

BILLY: That's all right, my girl. I dare say you know what you're doing. I should put your feet up, and close your eyes. You'll feel better in a minute.

JEAN: I had four gins. Four large gins. I'll be all right. What's the business like?

BILLY: At the theatre? I don't know. I don't ask. But I'll bet there's more in the saloon bar of the Cambridge than he's got in there. I know how you feel, girl. You just relax.

JEAN: I like listening to you. I always have.

BILLY: Yes, you always used to like coming to see me, didn't you? You used to enjoy yourself with me when you were a little girl. You were a pretty little thing. With your dark curls and your little dresses. (*Quickly.*) Not that looks are everything. Not even for a woman. Don't you believe it. You don't look at the mantelpiece when you poke the fire.

She sits down and leans back.

No, I'll say this for Archie—he always saw that you looked nicely turned out. You looked a little picture always. Spent too much I daresay. He was a smart little boy himself. Used to dress them in sailor suits then. He was a pretty little boy. Funny how they all turn out. (*Pause, then softly, sincerely*) I feel sorry for you people. You don't know what it's really like. You haven't lived, most of you. You've never known what it was like, you're all miserable really. You don't know what life can be like.

The light fades, a tatty backcloth descends.

NUMBER TWO

Front cloth. Darkened stage. Spotlight hits the prompt corner. Music strikes up. ARCHIE RICE makes his entrance.

23

ARCHIE: Good evening, ladies and gentlemen—Archie Rice is
the name. Archie Rice. Mrs. Rice's favourite boy.
We're going to entertain you for the next two and a
half hours and you've really had it now. All the exit
doors locked. Talking about being locked in, some of
these people ought to be locked up. Locked up. They
did, honest. I'll give you a case in point. A case in
point. My wife—my wife. Old Charlie knows her, don't
you, Charlie? Old Charlie knows her. A real road-
mender's job she is—isn't she, Charlie? It's all right.
I've taken his drill away from him now. I have.
Haven't I, Charlie. He's the only boy soprano in the
Musicians' Union. I know what you're waiting for. I
know what you're waiting for and who isn't? Just keep
your peckers up—they'll be on in a minute. You've got
to put up with me first. And now—now, to open the
show. I'm going to sing a little song I wrote myself. I
hope you like it.

> "Why should I care?
> Why should I let it touch me!
> Why shouldn't I, sit down and try
> To let it pass over me?
> Why should they stare,
> Why should I let it get me?
> What's the use of despair,
> If they call you a square?
> You're a long time dead——
> Like my pal Fred,
> So why, oh why should I bother to care?"

He goes into his dance routine.

> "Why should I care?
> Why should I let it touch me!
> Why shouldn't I, sit down and try
> To let it pass over me?
> Why should they stare,
> Why should I let it get me?
> What's the use of despair,
> If they call you a square?

> If they see that you're blue, they'll—look
>   down on you
>   So why should I bother to care? (Thank
>   God I'm normal!)
>   So why should I bother to care?"

EXIT

NUMBER THREE

The music fades. The backcloth goes up, revealing BILLY, JEAN and PHOEBE. PHOEBE is about sixty, with fair hair that was attractive once, and still has a great deal of care spent on it. Her face is made up, though not very skilfully. She is never still, she never listens—like most of the people in this house. Or, if she is obliged to sit and listen to anyone, she usually becomes abstracted and depressed, sitting on the edge of her chair, twisting her fingers round her hair. Just now, she is flushed, like a child, prepared to be excited.

PHOEBE: Oh, he will be so glad to see you. (*To Billy.*) Won't he? But why didn't you let us know? I'd have got you something prepared. Are you sure you won't have something? I've got a bit of York ham in—I bought it this morning. Wouldn't you like a bit of that?

JEAN: No thank you, dear. I told you I just came up on the spur of the moment.

PHOEBE: That's right, you did. But you said something in your letter about going away for the week-end. Did something go wrong?

JEAN: I changed my mind.

PHOEBE: Oh, well it's lovely to see you. Isn't it, Dad? He's pleased. He doesn't have anyone much to talk to. Do you? I say you don't have much chance for a talk. He's on his own here half the time. It's not my fault. He won't come to the pictures with me. But you've got to go somewhere, as I say to him. You get bored stiff just

25

sitting indoors. He likes to listen to a play on the wireless sometimes. You *like* a nice play. But I can't sit for long, I'd rather have a spot of pictures.

BILLY: I'm all right.

PHOEBE: Well, I suppose that's sitting down too, but it's not the same somehow, is it? Let's open this, shall we? (*She indicates bottle on the table.*) You shouldn't have bought gin. She's naughty, isn't she?

BILLY: She ought to have more sense—spending her money.

PHOEBE: Never mind, she's big hearted, that's the main thing. Hand me a couple of glasses. You're going to have one with me, aren't you? I don't want one on my own.

JEAN: All right—just a small one.

PHOEBE: Oh, sorry, Dad—do you want one?

BILLY: No thank you.

PHOEBE: Well, this is nice. What a shame—I'd have been in earlier but I stayed and saw a bit of the big picture round again.

BILLY: I know better than to overdo it.

JEAN: What was it like?

PHOEBE: The picture? Oh, wasn't up to much. But there was that nice fellow in it, what's his name? Oh, he sings sometimes, got very deep set eyes, dark. You'd know who I mean.

JEAN: Is he American or British?

PHOEBE: Oh, I don't know. American I should think.

JEAN: What was the picture called?

PHOEBE: (*laughs*). Blimey, you should know better than to ask me that! You know what a rotten memory I've got. Well, cheerio! (*She drinks.*) Oooh, that's a nice drop of gin—some of the muck they give you nowadays— tastes like cheap scent. You should hear him going on about the beer. No, they've a lot of rubbish on at the pictures these days. I haven't seen a decent picture for ages. It seems to be all bands or singing. Either that or Westerns. He doesn't mind them so much. But I can't stand all that shooting. It gives me a headache. But I'm dreadful—if there's nothing else on, I still go just the same, don't I? Even if it is just to the bug house round the corner. I get myself six penn'orth of sweets and have a couple of hours whatever's on. I hear they're closing that place down, by the way. Everything's doing badly. That's what I tell Archie. 'Course he gets worried because the business is bad. Still, that's how it is; people haven't got the money, have they? I'm at Woolworth's now, did I tell you? I'm on the electrical counter. It's not bad. Girls are a bit common, that's all. Oh, it is nice to see you. Archie will be so pleased. She looks a bit peaky. Round the face, don't you think? Don't you think she looks a bit peaky?

BILLY: She looks all right.

PHOEBE: I don't suppose she's eating properly. You know what these young girls are. They worry about their figures. So, you didn't go away for the week-end after all?

JEAN: No.

PHOEBE: Graham's all right, is he?

JEAN: Yes, he's all right.

PHOEBE: There's nothing wrong there, is there?

BILLY: Why don't you mind your bloody business? She'll tell you if she wants to.

PHOEBE: All right, I know. She doesn't mind telling me if there's anything, do you?

JEAN: We had a slight disagreement. Nothing more, that's all.

PHOEBE: After all, she may not be my own, but I did help to bring her up a little, didn't I? After all, she's Archie's daughter. Be a bit strange if I wasn't interested whether she was happy or not. Oh, well, dear, don't take any notice. You'll soon make it up. Men are funny. You don't want to take any notice of them.

JEAN: (smiling). Wish I didn't.

PHOEBE: That's right. Have another drink. You'll soon feel better. What did you have a row about? Something silly I'll bet. You haven't broken off your engagement?

JEAN: I don't know. Probably.

PHOEBE: Oh dear, I'm sorry.

JEAN: I went to the Rally in Trafalgar Square last Sunday.

BILLY: You did what?

JEAN: I went to the Rally in Trafalgar Square.

BILLY: What for, for God's sake?

JEAN: Because, Grandad, somehow—with a whole lot of other people, strange as it may seem—I managed to get myself steamed up about the way things were going.

BILLY: And you went to Trafalgar Square?

PHOEBE: Well she said so didn't she?

BILLY: Well I should think you want your bloody head read!

JEAN: That was more or less Graham's feeling about it. Only he happens to be about fifty years younger than you, and he put it a bit differently. It all really started over something I wanted to do, and then it all came out, lots of things. All kinds of bitterness—things I didn't even know existed.

BILLY: I didn't know you were interested in politics.

JEAN: Neither did I. I've always found the whole thing rather boring.

BILLY: Good God! I've heard some things in my time. This is what comes of giving them the bloody vote. They start breaking their engagements, just because they believe every shiftless lay-about writing for the papers.

PHOEBE: Oh, shut up, just for a minute, Dad. You had a row because of something you wanted to do?

JEAN: Well, it's—oh, it's a complicated story. I think I wrote and told you I was teaching Art to a bunch of Youth Club kids.

PHOEBE: Oh, yes. That was ages ago.

JEAN: Nearly a year. I knew someone who had been doing it—a young man Graham knew. He said it was too much for him, and he couldn't stick it any longer. "They're little bastards the lot of them," he said. "If anyone believes you can teach those monsters to create anything, they're crazy. They're a lot of little bastards." That's what he said. But—something, something, made me want to have a go at it. There wasn't any money in it. Just a few shillings for a few nights a week. But it was something I knew a little about—or thought I

28

knew about. I'd never been good enough to paint myself, but I thought this was something I really could do. Even if it was just battling a gang of moronic teenagers. The Club leader thought I was mad, and so did Graham.

PHOEBE: I can't say I blame him really. It doesn't sound a very nice job at all. Not for a young girl like you, Jean. They sound like a real tough crowd to me.

JEAN: They were. Too tough for either of the young men who had taken them on before.

PHOEBE: Well if they don't want to learn, why do they go for heaven's sake?

JEAN: It was an obligatory class, if they attended one of my classes a week, they could take part in the Club's other activities—the dances and so on. I fought those kids back—and some of them were eight feet tall. Most of the time I've loathed it, and I loathed them. I pretended to myself that I didn't, but I did. I hated them, but I think I was getting somewhere. And now Graham wants me to marry him. Now, before he's qualified but I wouldn't. He doesn't want me to try something for myself. He doesn't want me to threaten him or his world, he doesn't want me to succeed. I refused him. Then it all came out—Trafalgar Square and everything. You know, I hadn't realized—it just hadn't occurred to me that you could love somebody, that you could want them, and want them twenty-four hours of the day and then suddenly find that you're neither of you even living in the same world. I don't understand that. I just don't understand it. I wish I could understand it. It's frightening. Sorry, Phoebe, I shouldn't be drinking your gin. I bought this for you.

BILLY: Well we only need a few pigeons for it to be like Trafalgar Square in here. I've never known such a draughty bloody place. Everybody leaves the windows and doors open. I don't believe that's healthy. I tell you, you come in one door and you get blown out the other.

JEAN: How's young Mick—have you heard from him?

29

PHOEBE: Oh, yes. Of course. He's out there—you knew that, didn't you?

JEAN: Yes. I knew.

PHOEBE: Archie worries about him. He doesn't say so, but I know he does. It's funny really because they never seemed to hit it off so well, in lots of ways. Not like you and him, or Frank. He's a very sensible boy, young Mick. He's very straight. I've lost some sleep this week, I can tell you.

BILLY: He's a fine boy. When they called him, he went. No arguments, nothing. He just went.

JEAN: (*suddenly*). And when they called Frank, he refused, and he went to jail for it—for six months. Young Frank full of doubts about himself, and everybody, with a cold in his head half the year, and a weak chest. Lucky to pass C3. Poor Frank. (*To Phoebe.*) He's not very strong, you always said. You went without to buy him little luxuries to eat, why you wouldn't let him even clean his own shoes. No, you'd do it for him. But he went and said no, and, what's more, he went to jail for it. Oh, he gave in eventually, but he said no for six months of his poor protected life—he said no! I think that's something. You don't have to measure up young Mick against Frank, Grandad. Now, don't look hurt. I'm not getting at you. I love you very much—both of you, but I probably shouldn't have started drinking gin on the train.

Pause.

PHOEBE: Well, we'll shut up about it now.

BILLY: I just said that Mick was a good boy.

JEAN: He is. He's a very good boy. He's a gallant young nineteen year old who's fighting for us all, who never somehow learnt to say no, who never wanted to, and I hope to God he comes back safely.

PHOEBE: Oh dear, Jean, you think he'll be all right, don't you? I don't know why they send these boys out to do the fighting. They're just kids, that's all. That's all he is, a kid.

BILLY: You can't turn against your own people, Jean. You can't do it.

JEAN: Where is Frank? My own people—who are my people?

PHOEBE: He plays the piano in one of these late-night drinking places. He doesn't seem to know what to do with himself. Since he came out of that place. That damned prison. I'll never forget it. Making him go to prison. I'll never forget it. I can't get over it—ever.

JEAN: Well, it's all over now. Have some more of that gin. I bought it for you.

PHOEBE: I won't. And making him do that job. A boy like him shouldn't be doing it. Hospital porter. D'you know they made him stoke the boilers?

JEAN: Yes. He'd have been better off in the Army—sticking a bayonet into some wog.

PHOEBE: He doesn't say a word to me about it. I wish he hadn't done it all the same. I wonder whether Mick isn't better off after all. I mean—they do look after them, don't they?

JEAN: Oh, yes they look after them all right.

BILLY: Look after them better now than they did, when I was in it. I haven't read the evening paper yet. The Dardanelles—I went through that without a scratch. Not a scratch on me.

JEAN: They're all looking after us. We're all right, all of us. Nothing to worry about. *We're* all right. God save the Queen!

Blackout. Draw tabs.

NUMBER FOUR

Spotlight on ARCHIE at microphone.

ARCHIE: I've played in front of them all! "The Queen", "The Duke of Edinburgh", "The Prince of Wales", and the —what's the name of that other pub? Blimey, that went better first house. (*Pause.*) I've taken my glasses off. I don't want to see you suffering. What about these

31

crooners, eh? What about these crooners? I don't know what we're coming to. I don't, honest. Look at the stuff they sing. Look at the songs they sing! "The Dark Town Strutters' Ball", "The Woodchoppers' Ball", "The Basin' Street Ball"—it's a lot of rubbish, isn't it? I'll bet you thought I was a rotten act before I come on, didn't you? What about these girls? (*Indicates up stage*.) What about them? Smashin'. I bet you think I have a marvellous time up here with all these posing girls, don't you? You think I have a smashin' time don't you? (*Pause*.) You're dead right! You wouldn't think I was sexy to look at me, would you! No, lady. To look at me you wouldn't think I was sexy, would you! (*Pause*.) You ask him! (*Points to conductor's stand*.) Ask him! (*Staring out at audience*.) You think I'm like that, don't you? You think I am! Well, I'm not. But *he* is! (*Points to conductor's stand again*.) I'd rather have a glass of beer any day! And now I'm going to sing you a little song, a little song, a little song written by the wife's sister, a little song entitled "The Old Church bell won't ring tonight, as the Verger's dropped a clanger!" Thank you, Charlie.

> "We're all out for good old number one,
> Number one's the only one for me!
> Good old England, you're my cup of tea,
> But I don't want no drab equality.
> Don't let your feelings roam,
> But remember that charity begins at home.
> For Britons shall be free!
> The National Health won't bring you wealth
> Those wigs and blooming spectacles are
>   bought by you and me.
> The Army, the Navy and the Air Force,
> Are all we need to make the blighters see
> It still belongs to you, the old red, white and
>   blue

                Those bits of red still on the map
                We won't give up without a scrap.
                What we've got left back
                We'll keep—and blow you, Jack!
                Oh, number one's the only one for me!
                We're all out for good old number one,
                Yes number one's the only one for me——
                God bless you!
                Number one's the only one for me!
                Number one's the only one for me!"

                            EXIT

                    NUMBER FIVE

BILLY, PHOEBE, JEAN.

BILLY: They were graceful, they had mystery and dignity.
        Why when a woman got out of a cab, she descended.
        Descended. And you put your hand out to her smartly
        to help her down. Look at them today. Have you ever
        seen a woman get out of a car? Well, have you? I have,
        and I don't want to see it again, thank you very much.
        Why I never saw a woman's legs until I was nineteen.
        Didn't know what they looked like. Nineteen. I was
        married when I was nineteen, you know. I was only
        twenty when Archie's brother was born. Old Bill. He's
        got on, anyway. I remember the first time I set eyes on
        your grandmother. She was just eighteen. She had a
        velvet coat on, black it was, black with fur round the
        edge. They were all the fashion just about then. It was
        so tight round her figure. And with her little fur cap
        on and muff, she looked a picture.
        ARCHIE rushes in, his arms full with a carrier bag and
        bottles, briskly distracted. ARCHIE RICE is about fifty.
        His hair is brushed flat, almost grey. He wears glasses
        and has a slight stoop, from a kind of offhand pedantry

                            33

which he originally assumed thirty years ago when he left one of those minor public day schools in London, which have usually managed to produce some raffish middle class adventurers as well as bank managers and poets. Landladies adore and cosset him because he is so friendly, and obviously such a gentleman. Some of his fellow artists even call him "Professor" occasionally, as they might call a retired Army Captain "Colonel". He smiles kindly at this simplicity, knowing himself to belong to no class and plays the part as well as he knows how. He lightly patronizes his father, whom he admires deeply. He patronizes his wife, Phoebe, whom he pities wholeheartedly. It is this which has prevented him from leaving her twenty years ago. Or, is it simply because, as many people would suggest, he lacks the courage? Anyway, he makes no secret of his perennial affairs with other women—real and fictitious. It is part of his pity, part of his patronage, part of his personal myth. He patronizes his elder son Frank, who lacks his own brand of indulgence, stoicism and bravura, and for whom he has an almost unreal, pantomime affection. In contrast, his patronage of his daughter Jean is more wary, sly, unsure. He suspects her intelligence, aware that she may be stronger than the rest of them. Whatever he says to anyone is almost always very carefully "thrown away". Apparently absent minded, it is a comedian's technique, it absolves him seeming committed to anyone or anything.

ARCHIE: Ay, ay, women's legs again! (*To the others.*) That's what Sterne calls riding your tit with sobriety. I think it was Sterne, anyway. Or was it George Robey? Um? Hello, dear, this is nice. (*He kisses Jean.*) I haven't got my glasses on. I thought you were the Income Tax man sitting there. I thought we had shaken him off. All right, are you?

JEAN: Thank you. I have had too much gin waiting for you.

ARCHIE: Never mind, you can have some more in a minute. You haven't fixed an hotel or anything respectable, have you?

34

JEAN: No, but——

ARCHIE: Jolly good. I'm sleeping alone tonight. The back of my legs ache as it is. You and Phoebe can sleep up in my room, and I'll kip on the sofa. I've just been talking to our coloured friend on the stairs.

PHOEBE: He's a student.

ARCHIE: No he's not. He's a ballet dancer.

PHOEBE: (*astonished*). Is he! (*To Jean.*) He's a big fellow.

ARCHIE: Playing the Winter Gardens for a fortnight.

BILLY: A ballet dancer!

ARCHIE: He was telling me if you drop your hat outside there now, you have to kick it down to the promenade before you can pick it up. (*Pauses quickly, then goes on expertly.*) They're not all coloured, I saw a couple of 'em on the bus on the way home yesterday. They were talking together all the way, everybody listening. I just got up to press the bell, and a woman shouted out, "I lost two boys in the war for the likes of you!" I thought she meant me for a moment, so I turned round, and there she was, beating them with her umbrella like crazy.

BILLY: Don't like to see a man dancing like that.

ARCHIE: I was in a show with a couple of male dancers once. And wherever we went, on the Monday night some woman used to complain about their tights bulging. Wherever we went. Every Monday night. I'm sure it was the same woman each time. I used to call her the Camp Follower. Now, what are we going to have? Let's see what we've got. (*Rummages in carrier and pockets.*)

BILLY: There's a telegram come for you.

PHOEBE: Don't you think she's looking a bit peaky.

ARCHIE: Looks all right to me. Needs a drink that's all.

BILLY: (*beginning to get tired and irritable*). There's a telegram come for you!

ARCHIE: Have you been on the batter, you old gubbins!

BILLY: No I haven't! I've been sitting here talking to Jean.

ARCHIE: I should go to bed if you're tired.

BILLY: I'm not tired—I could see you out any day!

35

ARCHIE: (*picks up telegram*). You've been giving him that beastly gin. He sounds like a toast-master with DTs. One of my creditors. It'll wait. (*Throws it back on the table.*) You'd think they'd know better by this time! I've got some gin too—and dubonnet. Old Phoebe likes that don't you, dear! She thinks she's being awfully U when she drinks that, don't you?

PHOEBE: I like it. It seems to suit me. I can't drink gin on its own—not like he can. (*To Archie.*) What's all this for? Was it—was it all right at the theatre?

ARCHIE: No it wasn't all right at the theatre. Monday night there were sixty sad little drabs in, and tonight there were about two hundred sad little drabs. If we can open on Monday night at West Hartlepool, it will be by very reluctant agreement of about thirty angry people, but I'm not thinking about that tonight.

PHOEBE: Oh, Archie!

ARCHIE: Go on, have your dubonnet, dear. Don't get all emotional. Jean, that's yours. Billy, wake up!

BILLY: I am awake!

ARCHIE: Well stop yelling then. You're like one of those television commercials. There's a drink for you.

BILLY: I don't want a bloody drink.

ARCHIE: You look as though you're going to sing a hymn.

BILLY: I'm tired.

ARCHIE: Well that's better—have a drink and go to bed.

BILLY: I haven't seen the evening paper yet.

ARCHIE: Well if you've won the pools, we can read about it in the morning.

BILLY: I don't want to sit here and stagnate even if you do. I want to know what's going on in the world.

ARCHIE: Yes, you're amazingly well informed. (*To the others.*) He's quite well-read for an ignorant old pro.

BILLY: I'm not an ignorant old pro!

ARCHIE: Yes you are, now don't argue and drink up. I'm having a celebration.

BILLY: Celebration! What have you got to celebrate about?

ARCHIE: Oh dear.

BILLY: (*stands up*). You haven't got a thing you can call your
own. And as sure as God made little apples, I'll lay a
sovereign to a penny piece, you'll end up in the bank-
ruptcy court again before Christmas, and you'll be
lucky if you don't land up in jail as well.

PHOEBE: Get 'im to go to bed, Archie. He's over-tired.

ARCHIE: Go to bed. You're overtired.

BILLY: I'm not over-tired. I don't relish the idea of another
jail-bird in the family.

PHOEBE: Be quiet, Dad. You've had too much to drink.

BILLY: I could drink you lot under the table.

ARCHIE: Oh dear, he's getting religious now.

BILLY: I used to have half a bottle of three star brandy for
breakfast——

ARCHIE: And a pound of steak and a couple of chorus girls.
He'll tell you the whole story at the drop of a hat.

BILLY: (*in rage*). I leave chorus girls to *you*!

ARCHIE: Nothing like slicing yourself off a nice piece of bacon.

BILLY: I know what you mean.

ARCHIE: Don't get excited, Father. You'll wake the Poles up.

BILLY: Don't talk to me about that bunch of greasy tom-cats!
One Britisher could always take on half a dozen of that
kind. Or used to. Doesn't look like it now.

ARCHIE: Well never mind, don't spoil the party——

BILLY: I pay my way, which is more than you've ever done.
And I'll tell you that I was educated at one of the
finest schools in England.

ARCHIE: It produced one Field Marshal with strong Fascist
tendencies, one Catholic poet who went bonkers and
Archie Rice.

BILLY: D'you know what James Agate said about me?

ARCHIE: Oh yes—that you and Mrs. Pat Campbell were his
favourite female impersonators.

BILLY: You know bloody well what he said.
*Archie knows by long experience how far he can go and
he manages gently to turn the situation.*

ARCHIE: We all know what he said, and every word of it was true.
Billy glares at him, and grabs his glass.

37

ARCHIE: Well, as I was saying, before my ignorant old Father interrupted——

BILLY: There's nothing to be ashamed of in being an old pro. It's more than you'll ever be. You don't know the meaning of the word!

PHOEBE: Oh go to bed, Dad—you're getting silly now.

BILLY: You had to have personality to be a comedian then. You had to *really be somebody*!

ARCHIE: The reason for this little celebration is that tomorrow— oh it's today now—today is my twentieth anniversary.

PHOEBE: Twentieth anniversary? Anniversary of what?

ARCHIE: The twentieth anniversary of my not paying income tax. The last time I paid income tax was in 1936.

BILLY: They'll get you all right, they always get you in the end. You see!

ARCHIE: All right, love, you can sing us a hymn later. I think that is a very significant achievement, and I deserve some kind of tribute for it. (*To Jean.*) Don't you think your old man deserves a tribute?

JEAN: I was just wondering how you came to pay income tax in 1936.

ARCHIE: Bad luck that's all. I was trapped in hospital with a double hernia. Very nasty it was too. Terribly complicated. I even thought all my plans for the future were going to be finished at one point. Anyway, that's another story. I'll tell you sometime. I was lying there on my back, wondering whether draught Bass on its own was enough to make life worth living, when two men in bowlers and rain-coats sprang at me from behind the screens. That was Archie's one downfall. Could have happened to anyone. I think the ward-sister must have tipped them off. She used to tell me she was very spiritual, so she probably did. I'd gone legit. for a while just then, and I'd been in "The Tale of Two Cities". When I told her she said, "Oh, yes I think I've heard of that——" (*To Billy.*) She was an Irish lady. "A Tale of Two Cities—isn't it about Sodom and Gomorrah?" *Jean smiles. Billy and Phoebe are no longer listening.*

ARCHIE: A lady in the pit thought that was quite funny tonight.

PHOEBE: Jean's had an upset with Graham.

ARCHIE: Have you? Oh I'm sorry. I should have asked, shouldn't I? I'm sorry dear. I'm afraid I'm a wee bit slewed. (*Looks round.*) I think everyone is. You are.

PHOEBE: She's broken off her engagement.

ARCHIE: Have you really? Well, I should have thought engagements were a bit suburban for intellectuals like you anyway. You'll be getting a motor-cycle and side-car next.

PHOEBE: Oh stop poking fun at her, Archie. Be sensible. You can see she's upset.

JEAN: I'm not upset, and I haven't made a decision about anything yet. I just came up because I wanted to see you all, and see how you are. And because I miss you.

PHOEBE: Oh, did you really? That's very sweet of you, dear. I appreciate that, I do really.

ARCHIE: She knows I'm not poking fun at her.

PHOEBE: Oh, I wish I knew what's going to happen.

JEAN: Never mind about me. You haven't heard from young Mick?

ARCHIE: No, old Mick can look after himself, he's a boy without problems, that one. I expect he's screwing himself silly. I hope he is anyway. What's happened with you and Graham?

BILLY: Your daughter went to that Trafalgar Square circus last Sunday, if you please!

ARCHIE: Oh, really? Are you one of those who don't like the Prime Minister? I think I've grown rather fond of him. I think it was after he went to the West Indies to get Noel Coward to write a play for him. Still, perhaps only someone of my generation, could understand that. Does he bring you out in spots?

PHOEBE: Oh, Christ, I wish I knew what was going to happen to us!

ARCHIE: I feel rather like that about that horrible dog downstairs. It brings me out in a rash every time I look at it. There are three things that do that to me, three things. Nuns, clergymen and dogs.

PHOEBE: I don't want to always have to work. I mean you want a bit of life before it's all over. It takes all the gilt off if you know you've got to go on and on till they carry you out in a box. It's all right for him, he's all right. He's still got his women. While it lasts anyway. But I don't want to end up being laid out by some stranger in some rotten stinking little street in Gateshead, or West Hartlepool or another of those dead-or-alive holes!

JEAN: Phoebe don't upset yourself, please. Let's enjoy our-selves——

PHOEBE: Enjoy myself! D'you think I don't want to enjoy myself! I'm just sick of being with down and outs, I'm sick of it, and people like him.
She is crying.

ARCHIE: I wish women wouldn't cry. I wish they wouldn't. Try and say something to her, Jean.

JEAN: (*going to Phoebe*). Why don't you?

ARCHIE: I wish I could. I only wish I could.

JEAN: (*to Phoebe*). Come on, dear, would you like to go to bed?

PHOEBE: Yes, I think so, dear, if you don't mind. I think I've overdone it a bit. Archie knows what I'm like. I never could stand too much excitement. I think perhaps I got over-excited seeing you. It was such a nice surprise. And I'm probably worrying about young Mick under-neath. I keep thinking of all that fighting——

ARCHIE: Get some sleep, love, you'll feel better when you wake up.

PHOEBE: (*rising*). All right, dear. I'll get along, it's late anyway. Dad should have been in bed hours ago. He'll be awful tomorrow. Make him go to bed, Archie, will you?

ARCHIE: I will. (*To Jean.*) See her up.

PHOEBE: (*stopping*). Would you come and say good night to me, Archie?

ARCHIE: Yes. I'm just going to finish my little celebration. It's my anniversary, remember?

PHOEBE: (*smiles*). He's funny.
Exit with Jean.

ARCHIE: (*to Billy*). Want another before you turn in?

BILLY: No thank you. I have had sufficient.

ARCHIE: Go on you old gubbins. (*Pours out a drink.*) I know that expression. That's your hymn look.

BILLY: You think I won't!

ARCHIE: I'm damn sure you will. All right, let's have a good heart warmer. Then drink up your beer and go to bed.

BILLY: All right. I will.

He sits upright and sings.

> "Onward Christian soldiers
> Marching as to war
> With the Cross of Jesus
> Going on before.
> Christ the Royal Master
> Fights against the foe
> Forward into battle . . ."

Jean has come back into the room and Billy is too weary to go on. He starts to move down to his room.

BILLY: Good night, Jean. It was good to see you. We'll have a talk tomorrow.

JEAN: Yes, we will. And you're taking me to the Club, remember.

BILLY: Good night, son.

ARCHIE: Good night, Dad.

Exit Billy.

JEAN: Dad——

ARCHIE: Yes.

JEAN: You're keeping something to yourself.

ARCHIE: You never miss a thing, do you? Observation—is the basis of all Art.

JEAN: What is it? I've had a strange sick feeling in my stomach all day. As if something was going to happen. You know the feeling.

ARCHIE: Yes. I know the feeling. Mick's been taken prisoner. Nobody here seemed to know. It's in the paper actually. There was no point in breaking it tonight. Tomorrow's soon enough. (*He tears open the telegram.*) They usually get these things before the people who

41

really matter. I knew what this must be. (*He hands it to her and picks up the paper.*) He seems to have been shooting up quite a lot of wogs, doesn't he? There's a picture of your friend here too, the one who gives you a rash. He's looking rather serious this time. Perhaps he's worrying about young Mick.

JEAN: I think I will have some of that.

He pushes her glass towards her.

ARCHIE: Well, Mick wouldn't want us to cut the celebration short. We'll drink to Mick, and let's hope to God he manages. Mick and the income tax man. With you it's Prime Ministers, with me it's dogs. Nuns, clergymen and dogs. Did I ever tell you the greatest compliment I had paid to me—the greatest compliment I always treasure? I was walking along the front somewhere—I think it was here actually—one day, oh, it must be twenty-five years ago, I was quite a young man. Well, there I was walking along the front, to meet what I think we used to call a piece of crackling. Or perhaps it was a bit of fluff. No that was earlier. Anyway, I know I enjoyed it afterwards. But the point is I was walking along the front, all on my own, minding my own business, (*Pause*) and two nuns came towards me—(*Pause*) two nuns——

He trails off, looking very tired and old. He looks across at Jean and pushes the bottle at her.

ARCHIE: Talk to me.

CURTAIN

END OF ACT ONE

INTERMISSION

BILLY, PHOEBE and JEAN. PHOEBE is flushed with drink.

BILLY: I knew they couldn't keep him. They wouldn't dare.

PHOEBE: Home in a couple of days—I just can't believe it.

BILLY: They wouldn't dare, not even nowadays—cock-eyed bunch they are. I remember 'em from before the war. I was with that show, you remember, Phoebe——

PHOEBE: Well what would they want to keep a boy like that for? That's what I kept asking myself. Can't do them any good. It couldn't do them any good, could it?

BILLY: Grubby lot of rogues. I was a guest at the Ambassadors, you know. Gave me a box of Romeo and Juliet cigars.

JEAN: (*surrounded by pile of newspapers*). Well, the name of Rice is famous once again.

BILLY: This long they were. Haven't had a cigar like that for years.

PHOEBE: He likes a cigar. I buy those cheroots sometimes. They're only cheap things, but he doesn't mind them, does he?

BILLY: Course I don't mind them. Jeannie gave me some didn't she? What's the matter with you?

PHOEBE: Oh yes I was forgetting.

BILLY: Got a mind like a bloody sieve!

PHOEBE: I was always a dunce at school. I keep thinking of Archie. I'm so afraid that he's going to be disappointed. That everything will go wrong, and they won't let Mick come home after all.

BILLY: Pardon me, Phoebe, but you do talk the most almighty rubbish I've ever had to sit and listen to.

JEAN: They've given a formal undertaking.

BILLY: Formal undertaking, my backside—if I thought that boy's future depended on their "formal undertaking" we could say "thank you very much and good night".

PHOEBE: (*paper in her lap*). We've got an aeroplane standing by all ready to rush him home.

BILLY: "Formal undertaking"—proper politicians' words they are. They'd mean damn all if they were said by one of ours.

JEAN: (*reading*). "Bring him home"—in a matter of a few hours Sergeant Rice should be speeding homewards in a specially allocated Dakota.

BILLY: They know damn well they daren't do anything else.

JEAN: We're going to have ourselves a hero, you can see that——

BILLY: Any one of us would have done the same thing. There's nothing wrong with any of us, never has been. You can't all get to the top. You can't make your own luck. Me, I was always lucky, always was. Mind you, I was good too. That Ambassador, Sir Somebody Pearson his name was, charming, absolutely, the real best type, absolutely the best type. He told me I was his favourite artist. Barring George Robey.

PHOEBE: What good would it do them, hanging on to a kid. That's all he is.

JEAN: This one says——

BILLY: He's lucky. I was always lucky. Mind you, I was good too.

JEAN: (*reading*). "Lieut. Pearson, of Leicester, who had been with Sergeant Rice until a few minutes before he was captured, said he must have killed at least seven of the attackers."

BILLY: Was that Pearson you said——

JEAN: "Before he was overwhelmed, 'he must have run out of ammunition' said Pearson. Young Rice wasn't the type to give up."
Pause.

PHOEBE: I don't want Archie to be disappointed, that's all. On top of everything else. He's had enough of disappointments. I don't think he ever really gets used to them.

BILLY: You see, a couple of days, and Mick'll be sitting down here talking about it.

PHOEBE: I remember once my Mum promised to take us kids to the pantomime, and then something happened, she couldn't take us. I don't know what it was, she didn't have the money I expect. You could sit up in the gallery then for sixpence. Poor old Mum—she took us later, but it didn't seem the same to me. I was too disappointed. I'd been thinking about that pantomime for weeks. You shouldn't build things up. You're always disappointed really. That's Archie's trouble. He always builds everything up. And it never turns out.

BILLY: He's a fool.

PHOEBE: He's too good for them, that's his trouble. People don't appreciate you properly. Let's finish this up shall we? Archie'll bring some more in with him when he comes.

BILLY: It's all over, finished. I told him years ago. But he won't listen. He won't listen to anybody.

PHOEBE: You can't help giving Archie his own way. Not really. No, all they're out for is a cheap thrill. (*To Jean.*) Come on, have half of this with me. We've all got to—what's the word?

BILLY: I dunno what you're talking about.

JEAN: Compromise?

PHOEBE: She knows what I mean. That's right, dear. You keep on and on, try your best, and then a time comes when you can't go on any longer. It's not giving in—or I suppose it is. It's just being sensible. (*To Jean.*) Has he said anything to you?

JEAN: What about?

PHOEBE: Oh, about anything. He never tells me anything now, he just tells me not to worry, and says nothing. Frank told me the company only got half salary on Saturday night, and he thinks these scenery people must have caught up with him because——

BILLY: He said he'd bring me back some cigarettes. I could have got them myself by this time. I suppose he's in that Rockliffe.

PHOEBE: Whenever there's a ring at the door, I daren't answer it, in case it's a policeman standing there with another summons.

JEAN: (*offering cigarettes to Billy*). Have one of these.

BILLY: That bloody meat market.

PHOEBE: It's not a nice feeling when you can't go and answer the door.

BILLY: There'll be a policeman at the door all right——

PHOEBE: (*weary, not peevish*). Oh, don't keep interrupting while I'm talking to Jean.

BILLY: (*to Jean, politely*). Thank you, my dear. (*Picks up his newspaper.*)

PHOEBE: I've upset him now.

JEAN: No you haven't. He's just reading. Aren't you, Grandad?

BILLY: Um?

PHOEBE: Oh well, it's no good worrying. Is it? It says in the papers Mick's coming home, and they ought to know about these things, and that's all that really matters. Have a drop of this, dear.

BILLY: No thank you.

PHOEBE: (*to Jean*). Pour him out a glass. There's one over there. Oh, Dad, he exaggerates everything, don't you? He exaggerates everything, but he's right, you know. He's right about Archie. He hasn't got an enemy in the world who's done him the harm he's done himself.

JEAN: There you are, Grandad.

BILLY: Thank you, Jean. I'll have it later.

JEAN: Don't have it later. Have it now. This is the time to celebrate. Come on then. Let's drink to Mick.

PHOEBE: Yes, we mustn't sit here, getting morbid. We're a bit short on the drink, aren't we? I hope Archie won't be long in that place.

JEAN: Frank's gone with him. He won't be long.

PHOEBE: Oh, Frank'll see he doesn't get home too late. Frank's a sensible boy—sometimes he is anyway. (*To Jean.*) I think you're the only really sensible one of us lot.

JEAN: Grandad doesn't think so, do you?

BILLY: She's just as bloody daft as the rest of you.

PHOEBE: He's a fool to himself. Always some big idea he's got to

46

make money. A while back it was female impersonators. We were going to make a packet. That's what Archie said anyway. But by the time Archie got started with it it had all petered out. Now it's rock and roll. Oh well. It's like the women. They get tired of him. They come back here a few times, and that's that——

BILLY: Why don't you hold your bloody noise!

PHOEBE: He doesn't like me talking about it. As if she didn't know what's been going on all this time.

BILLY: Well there's no reason to talk about it.

PHOEBE: She's not soft, are you, dear?

BILLY: I don't want to hear about it, and I shouldn't think she does.

PHOEBE: All right, all right.

BILLY: She's used to be with people who know how to behave. She doesn't want to hear about your troubles.

PHOEBE: No of course she doesn't.

BILLY: Well then—the trouble with you people is you don't know how to carry on properly, that's your trouble. Give the girl a chance, she's got her own life to lead.

PHOEBE: I was only telling her——

BILLY: And I'm telling you don't! There's nothing *you* can tell her. So hold your noise——

JEAN: Grandad, please——

BILLY: Why don't you go back to London to your friends?

JEAN: Don't let's argue——

BILLY: We're no good to you——

JEAN: I don't think I want to go back to London——

PHOEBE: I was only talking to her about Archie. You don't want to leave, do you, dear?

JEAN: Of course I don't.

PHOEBE: I was just saying, in the course of ordinary conversation, that Archie wasn't very lucky that's all.

JEAN: Here—(*She has put a small bottle of gin on the table.*)

PHOEBE: And if I mention the women, it was just because it's been the same thing with them. It's never bothered me, that, so much. It never meant a great deal to me, not even when I was young. Still, I suppose men are

47

different. It's more important to them. Oh, look what she's done!

JEAN: I thought I'd better get some in, in case Dad was late.

BILLY: What do you think you're supposed to be—a millionairess?

JEAN: But you're not to have any, till you've had something to eat first, you've had nothing but tea and cigarettes for days.

PHOEBE: I couldn't eat anything, dear. Honestly.

JEAN: I'll get something for you.

PHOEBE: No, I couldn't. I couldn't—hold it down.

JEAN: (*moving*). I'm not going to argue——

PHOEBE: Jean, I've asked you—I can't! I don't want it!

JEAN: But people have got to eat, dear. If you don't have something——

PHOEBE: (*laughing slightly*). People have to eat, she says. That's a good one!

JEAN: You can't carry on, dear.

Billy gets up humming "Rock of Ages" and goes off L.

PHOEBE: People have to eat, she says. D'you hear that? Where's he got to?

JEAN: He's just gone into the kitchen.

PHOEBE: That's not all they have to do. They have to do a whole lot of things, a lot of things you don't even know about, and it's nothing to do with being educated and all that. Why should you know about it?

JEAN: I know, love. Things have been tough. But be sensible, you've got to keep on.

PHOEBE: Don't tell me to be sensible, Jean.

JEAN: I'm sorry, dear. I didn't mean it like that——

PHOEBE: Don't tell me to be sensible! You're a sweet girl, Jean, and I'm very fond of you. But you're not even my own daughter. I wouldn't take that from Mick or Frank, and they're my own.

JEAN: All right, forget it. We'll forget it. We haven't had our drink to Mick yet.

PHOEBE: Don't—don't presume too much.

JEAN: Phoebe please—I just——

48

PHOEBE: Don't presume too much. What's he doing out there?

JEAN: He's probably getting him something to eat, I expect.

PHOEBE: I don't want him messing about out there. He knows I don't like him going out there. He leaves everything in such a mess.

JEAN: Here, have this.

PHOEBE: Why doesn't Archie come back? You'd think he'd come back here and celebrate after hearing his son is safe and on his way home. I don't know—you people——

JEAN: Come along, Phoebe, don't let's have a row. And over nothing—it's silly.

PHOEBE: It's not silly. Anyway, who said we're having a row? All I said was I wasn't hungry, and you start getting at me.

JEAN: I wasn't getting at you.

PHOEBE: You people—you're all alike.

JEAN: Believe me, Phoebe. I wasn't——

PHOEBE: I can't eat because I feel sick.

JEAN: Well, all right then.

PHOEBE: You don't know what it's like. You don't know what it's like because we tried to do our best by you. Oh, Archie tried to do his best by you, even if it didn't add up to very much. Not that you weren't a good girl, you worked hard. You deserved it, you've always tried, and you've got what it takes. And that's more than any of us have got, my dear. You're the only one of us who has. You and young Mick. And the old man of course. He had it. Not that it's any use to him now. He's just a has-been, I suppose. Still—it's better to be a has-been than a never-was. His other son's the same—Old Bill. Archie's brother. Not that you'd think he was. Now he's really a big pot. He's really a big pot. There's no flies on brother Bill.

JEAN: (*trying to turn the conversation*). He's a barrister—that's why you like him so much. He's like that actor on the pictures who's always in a wig and gown in every other——

PHOEBE: I like him because he's a gentleman. He's different

49

from your father, even if they did go to the same posh
school and all that. I like him because of the way he
treats me. He talks to me beautifully, the way he calls
me "Phoebe". You should hear the way he calls me
"Phoebe".

JEAN: I only saw him a couple of times.

PHOEBE: Well, of course you did. He didn't approve of the way
Archie carried on. He never did. Sometimes, in the early
days he'd come and see us. He always slipped a couple
of fivers in my hand before he left, and he'd just say
"Not a word to Archie, now". I just never used to know
what to say to him. We'd always be living in some
bloody digs somewhere, and I didn't like him coming.
I'd feel awful. He could never bring his wife, and I
never knew what to say. Then he and Archie would
always have a row over something Archie had been
doing. Either he'd lost money, or he was out of work.
I remember he came once, and Archie and me didn't
have a bean. We'd been living on penny pieces of bacon
from the butcher's, and what we got then from the
Tribunal. (*She pronounces it Tribbunel.*) You and the
boys were staying with the Old Man then. Archie
wouldn't take money from his Dad then—perhaps it was
professional jealousy, I don't know. Anyway, Bill heard
that Archie was in trouble again—I don't remember
what it was. But it was something serious this time, I
think. Oh, he tried to pass a dud cheque and he'd
picked the wrong person or something. That wasn't like
Archie, I must admit, because he never did anything
really dishonest like that, whatever else he might have
done. He must have been drunk. Anyway, Old Bill
came over—we were living at Brixton at that time, and
the kids in the street made a terrible mess of his car.
They didn't see many cars in that street except when it
was the doctor. Not that he said a word about it. When
we went to the door, and I saw what they'd done to it,
I just stood there, I felt so ashamed, and I burst out
crying. He patted my arm in that way of his and he just

said "I'm so sorry, Phoebe. I really am. I'm afraid it's always going to be like this". Well, he got Archie out of whatever it was, and that was that. It wasn't the money, or his helping Archie—although I was grateful for that, of course. It was the way he spoke to me in that quiet gentlemanly way, and the way he patted my arm.

JEAN: Yes, I can see him doing it.

PHOEBE: What do you mean—what do you mean by that remark?

JEAN: Oh nothing, dear. Let's not talk about it——

PHOEBE: What do you mean by that remark?

JEAN: Oh, it's just that I can see brother Bill patting your arm, slipping that ten pounds in your hand, and then driving off to have dinner at his Club. That's all, Phoebe. Now let's not talk about it any more.

PHOEBE: You mean he was just sorry for me, don't you?

JEAN: No, I don't.

PHOEBE: Come on, say it—you mean he was just sorry for me, don't you?

JEAN: I didn't say that and I didn't mean that. Now come on——

Enter ARCHIE with FRANK. FRANK is a pale, shy boy of about nineteen. He has allowed himself to slip into the role of ARCHIE's "feed" because this seems to be a warm, reasonable relationship substitute that suits them both. He is impulsive, full of affection that spills over easily. He is young, and will probably remain so.

PHOEBE: I want to know what you meant.

ARCHIE: My dear, nobody can tell you what they mean. You ought to know that by now.

PHOEBE: Shut up a minute, Archie—I'm talking to Jean. She knows what I mean. You know what I meant, don't you?

ARCHIE: Do you know what she means? I wish to God I did. (*To Frank.*) I can see we should have stayed.

PHOEBE: Shall I tell you something?

JEAN: Phoebe, what are you doing?

PHOEBE: Shall I?

JEAN: It's just that I know exactly how Uncle Bill patted your

arm—just in the same way as he'd wait on the men at
Christmas when he was in the army. So democratic, so
charming, and so English.

ARCHIE: Oh, Bill's all right. Just doesn't understand people like
us, that's all. And what's more he doesn't want to.
Can't blame him really.

PHOEBE: (*to Jean*). You don't like him, do you? I knew you
didn't like him.

ARCHIE: Like now. Oh, brother Bill wouldn't understand all this
at all. He'd be frightfully embarrassed, wouldn't he?
Give us over that carrier, Frankie love.

PHOEBE: You can't afford not to like him. You owe him too
much.

ARCHIE: Sounds a pretty good reason for not liking anyone, I
should say.

PHOEBE: He's something you'll never be.

ARCHIE: And I'm something he'll never be—good Old Bill. He
may be successful, but he's not a bad sort. Do you
know that my brother Bill has had one wife, no love
affair, he's got three charming gifted children. Two of
them took honours degrees at Cambridge, and all of
them have made what these people call highly successful marriages.

FRANK: What on earth's everybody talking about? Hullo, Jean,
love. I thought we were going to have a party.
He throws his arms around her and kisses her.

ARCHIE: It's perfectly true. I read it in the *Telegraph* today. I
got bored reading about young Mick, and there, tucked
away in the middle——

JEAN: (*eagerly*). Don't tell me you read——

ARCHIE: Of course, I read it. How else would I know whether
my relations were getting married, or dying, or having
babies. As I was saying——

FRANK: Before you were so rudely interrupted.
Kissing Jean affectionately once again.

ARCHIE: Yes, before that. Young Sonia is getting married.

JEAN: Who to?

ARCHIE: Oh, the son of some industrialist, Capt. Charlie

Double-back-Action hyphen-breech loading Gore of Elm Lodge, Shrewkesbury, Glos. Where are all the glasses, for God's sake? Good ole Bill—he's got everything he wants now, including Captain Charlie Double-back-Action Gore.

PHOEBE: Archie, I'm talking to Jean.

ARCHIE: Yes, I thought that's what you were doing. I sized the situation up in a flash.

PHOEBE: Oh, it's easy for people like you to make fun. I left school when I was twelve years old.

ARCHIE: Christ, if she tells me that once more I shall get up on the roof, drunk as I am, I shall get up on the roof and scream. I've never done that before.

PHOEBE: You had to pay sixpence a week then.

FRANK: Leave her alone, you old bastard. Come on, Mum, we're going to have a party.

PHOEBE: I'm talking to Jean.

ARCHIE: Yes, we were in on that. Why don't we all talk to Jean. We don't see much of her. Frank—talk to Jean.

FRANK: Dad——

He nods towards PHOEBE, distressed to see her like this, but ARCHIE, who has come in prepared to be gay, is tired and has begun to give up the situation.

ARCHIE: Let's have a drink first. If I'm going to be either very diplomatic, or very tactful, I must have plenty to drink first.

PHOEBE: We had to pay sixpence a week, and most weeks my mother couldn't find it——

ARCHIE: This is a welfare state, my darling heart. Nobody wants, and nobody goes without, all are provided for.

PHOEBE: I was out scrubbing a dining hall for——

ARCHIE: Everybody's all right. Young Mick's all right. Bill's all right. Why, he never even got himself jailed by a lot of wogs. Frank's all right—he won't be stoking boilers much longer, will you, boy?

FRANK: I wish you'd both shut up.

ARCHIE: Jean's all right. She'll make it up with Graham, and forget about silly old Trafalgar Square, and Prime

53

Ministers who look like dogs downstairs. Here you are, dear. (*Offers drink to Phoebe.*)

PHOEBE: You don't understand——

ARCHIE: I know. Phoebe scrubbed a dining hall floor for five hundred kids when she was twelve years old, didn't you?

PHOEBE: Oh——

ARCHIE: Didn't you? Have you any idea, any of you, have you any idea how often she's told me about those five hundred kids and that dining hall?

FRANK: Oh, shut up.

ARCHIE: Yes, son, I'll shut up. Pass this to Jean. She looks as though she can use it.
(*Rises and gives drink to Jean. Remain standing by D.L. chair.*)

JEAN: I can.

FRANK: You've been away too long. Every night is party night.

ARCHIE: And do you know why? Do you know why? Because we're dead beat and down and outs. We're drunks, maniacs, we're crazy, we're bonkers, the whole flaming bunch of us. Why, we have problems that nobody's ever heard of, we're characters out of something that nobody believes in. We're something that people make jokes about, because we're so remote from the rest of ordinary everyday, human experience. But we're not really funny. We're too boring. Simply because we're not like anybody who ever lived. We don't get on with anything. We don't ever succeed in anything. We're a *nuisance*, we do nothing but make a God almighty fuss about anything we ever do. All the time we're trying to draw someone's attention to our nasty, sordid, unlikely little problems. Like that poor, pathetic old thing there. Look at her. What has she got to do with people like you? People of intellect and sophistication. She's very drunk, and just now her muzzy, under-developed, un-trained mind is racing because her blood stream is full of alcohol I can't afford to give her, and she's going to force us to listen to all sorts of dreary embarrassing things we've all heard a hundred times before. She's getting old, and she's worried about who's going to keep her when she can't work any longer. She's afraid of ending up in a long box in somebody else's front room in Gateshead, or was it West Hartlepool?

PHOEBE: What's he talking about?

ARCHIE: She's going to tell you that old brother Bill paid for all your education. That's what she wants to tell you, Jean. That scholarship didn't pay for the things that really mattered, you know. The books, the fares, the clothes, and all the rest of it. Bill paid for that. For all of you. Frank knows that, don't you, Frank? I'm sorry, Phoebe. I've killed your story. Old Archie could always kill anybody's punch line if he wanted.

PHOEBE: She doesn't know about Mick and you and me. I know she doesn't.

ARCHIE: She'll find out. We always find these things out in time. (*To Frank and Jean.*) She's tired and she's getting old. She's tired, and she's tired of me. Nobody ever gave her two pennyworth of equipment except her own pretty unimpressive self to give anything else to the rest of the world. All it's given her is me, and my God she's tired of that! Aren't you, my old darling? You're tired of that, aren't you?

PHOEBE: (*fiercely*). I tried to make something of myself. I tried, I really did try. I was nothing much to look at, but what I was I made myself. I was a plain kid—no I wasn't. I wasn't even plain. I was the ugliest bloody kid you ever saw in your life. You've never seen anyone as ugly as I was. But I made something of myself. I did try to do something. I made him want me anyway.

FRANK: Everyone shouts! Please, somebody speak quietly, just for once. Those bloody Poles will be up here in a minute. Let's have a row. It looks as if we're going to have one anyway. But please can we have a *quiet* row!

ARCHIE: It was a long time ago. They knew it was a long time ago. (*To Frank.*) I wish you'd stop yelling, I can't hear myself shout. Sing one of your songs, there's a good boy. Where's the old man?

55

JEAN: He's in the kitchen.

ARCHIE: Billy! Come out of there! Who's he got in there? Something you picked up in the Cambridge! Have you ever had it on a kitchen table? Like a piece of meat on a slab. Slicing pieces of bacon. Don't you wish you were back with old Graham? (*To Jean.*)

PHOEBE: Frank, he's going to bring up one of those women, isn't he? In here, isn't he?

ARCHIE: Leave her alone, son.
Sits L. of D.R. sofa.

PHOEBE: Do you think I don't lie awake upstairs, and hear it going on?

ARCHIE: Of course they know. They know what sort of a bastard I am, love. I think they know almost as well as you do. Well, almost as well. She'll be all right, won't you, love? Where's the old man? (*To Frank and Jean.*) Now don't pretend you're not used to it.
Billy appears.
There you are, you old has-been! Have you brought us a slice of bacon in?

BILLY: What's the matter with you lot?

ARCHIE: We're all just waiting for the little yellow van to come——

BILLY: Did you get my cigarettes?

ARCHIE: Except for Jean. There's still hope for her. You wait, you old Gubbins, you'll be reading about your grand-daughter and Mr. Graham Thing of Elm Lodge, Shrewkesbury, Glos. Here you are. (*Tosses cigarettes to Billy and gives him a drink.*)

PHOEBE: (*to Billy*). You've been at that cake.

BILLY: What?

PHOEBE: You've been at my cake. You've been at my cake, haven't you?

BILLY: (*flushing*). I was hungry——

PHOEBE: That cake was for Mick. It was for Mick, it wasn't for you.

BILLY: I'm sorry——

PHOEBE: I bought it for Mick. It was for when he comes home.

56

ARCHIE: Well, never mind.

PHOEBE: What do you mean—never mind!

ARCHIE: Mick wouldn't mind.

PHOEBE: Well I mind! I don't want him in that kitchen. Tell him to keep out of it. It's not much, and it's not mine, but I mind very much. Why couldn't you leave it alone?

BILLY: I just fancied——

PHOEBE: Couldn't you leave it alone? It wasn't for you. What's the matter with you? I feed you, don't I? Don't think you give me all that much money every week, because you don't!

ARCHIE: Phoebe, forget it!

PHOEBE: I don't forget, I don't forget anything. I don't forget anything even if you do.

ARCHIE: We'll buy another one.

PHOEBE: Oh, you'll buy another one! You're so rich! You're such a great big success! What's a little cake—we'll order a dozen of 'em! I bought that cake, and it cost me thirty shillings, it was for Mick when he comes back, because I want to give him something, something I know he'll like, after being where he's been, and going through what he has—and now, that bloody *greedy* old pig—that old pig, as if he hadn't had enough of everything already—he has to go and get his great fingers into it!

Unable to top this, she bursts into tears. BILLY stands, ashamed and deeply hurt by what she has said, even though he vaguely realizes the condition she is in. He puts down the drink he has been holding, and the cigarettes.

BILLY: Excuse me, Jean.

He crosses down to his room and goes out.

PHOEBE: Archie, you haven't got anybody coming tonight, have you?

ARCHIE: I suppose he has had more than any of us, and he's enjoyed it. Good luck to him. All the same, you needn't have done that. No, there's nobody coming.

PHOEBE: Oh, I'm sorry, Archie. Try and forgive me——

ARCHIE: Not that I don't wish there were. But then you know that. Come on love, pull yourself together. That's what we should have done years ago. Pulled ourselves together. Let's pull ourselves together. (*Sings.*) Let's pull ourselves together, together, together. Let's pull ourselves together, and the happier we'll be!

FRANK: That's right chaps—remember we're British!

ARCHIE: That's what everybody does. Perfectly simple. I've always known it. That's what my old brother Bill used to tell me. Now let's fill up and be happy. What about old Mick, eh?

FRANK: Yes, what about old Mick? Don't look so glum, Jean. You know what everybody's like.

JEAN: Do I?

ARCHIE: Never mind, there's no reason why she should, as Phoebe would say. We're all a bit slewed, which means that we're a bit more sub-human even than we usually are. (*To Frank.*) Isn't that right, you great weedy boiler stoker you! I'll bet the patients in that hospital all freeze to death—he must be saving the National Health thousands.

FRANK: (*to Phoebe*). Feel all right now?

PHOEBE: Perhaps Jean doesn't want to have a drink, and do you know why?

ARCHIE: No, why?

PHOEBE: Because I don't think she even likes him. I don't think she likes Mick.

ARCHIE: There's no reason why she should. But that won't stop her. Or me. Frank, go in and talk to the old man, and get him to come back. (*Crosses to D.R. proscenium arch.*) We'll try to be a little normal just for once, and pretend we're a happy, respectable, decent family. For Mick's sake. You know, I really think that's what he'd like, somehow. I'm sure he thinks we're rather dreadful. Worse than the wogs really. Don't worry, Jean, you won't have to put up with this kind of thing for long— any more than Mick. And this is Mick's party. Phoebe, let's see you do your dance. (*This is thrown off in the*

58

usual casual, studied Archie manner.) She dances jolly
well, don't you, you poor old thing. I wonder if she'll
make me cry tonight. We'll see. We'll see. Frank, sing
us your song.

JEAN: I don't even know what I'm feeling. I don't even know
if I do at all.

ARCHIE: Never mind, dear. I didn't know that for years, either.
You're a long time dead, Mrs. Murphy, let's make it a
party, Mick the soldier's coming back, let's just whoop
it up!

CURTAIN

NUMBER SEVEN

Music. ARCHIE rises, his face held open by a grin, and
dead behind the eyes. Just now and then, for a second
or two, he gives the tiniest indication that he is almost
surprised to find himself where he is.

ARCHIE: Here, here! Here, I've just seen a man with a lemon
stuck in his ear! A lemon stuck in his ear! So I went up
to him, I said: "What are you doing with that lemon
stuck in your ear?" and he says: "Well, you know that
man with a hearing aid—well, I'm the man with the
lemonade." Thank you for that burst of heavy breath-
ing. You should have heard what James Agate said
about *me*! (*Back again.*) But I have a go, lady, don't I?
I 'ave a go. I do. You think I am, don't you? Well, I'm
not. But *he* is! Here, here! Did I tell you about the
wife? Did I? My wife—not only is she stupid, not only
is she stupid, but she's cold as well. Oh yes, cold. She
may look sweet, but she's a very cold woman, my wife.
Very cold. Cold and stupid. She's what they call a
moron glacee. Don't clap too hard—it's a very old
building. Well, I 'ave a go, don't I? I do—I 'ave a go.
Look at me—it's all real, you know. Me—all real,
nothing shoddy. You don't think I'm real, do you?
Well, I'm not. (*Stumbling.*) I'm not going to deprive

59

you of the treat I know you've all been waiting for.
Yes, I'm going to sing to you. I'm going to sing to you
a little song, a little song written by myself. I haven't
recorded it, so if you like it, you tell 'em. They won't
listen, but you tell 'em. A little song called "My girl's
always short of breath, but she don't mind a good blow
through."
He sings.

> Now I'm just an ordinary bloke
> The same as you out there.
> Not mad for women, I'm not a soak,
> I never really care.
> I'm what you call a moderate,
> I weigh all the pros. and the cons.
> I don't push and shove
> At the thing they call love,
> I never go in for goings on.
> Thank God I'm normal, normal, normal.
> Thank God I'm normal,
> I'm just like the rest of you chaps.

> Thank God I'm normal,
> I'm just like the rest of you chaps,
> Decent and full of good sense,
> I'm not one of these extremist saps,
> For I'm sure you'll agree,
> That a fellow like me
> Is the salt of our dear old country,
>   of our dear old country.

Bang on appropriate lighting. Speaking:

> But when our heritage is threatened
> At home or cross the sea.

Play "Land of Hope and Glory".

> It's chaps like us—yes you and me,
> Who'll march again to victory.
> Some people say we're finished,
> Some people say we're done.
> But if we all stand

60

Spotlight behind gauze reveals a nude in Britannia's helmet and holding a bulldog and trident.

> By this dear old land,
> The battle will be won.
>
> Thank God we're normal, normal, normal.
> Thank God we're normal.
> We are the country's flower,
> And when the great call comes,
> Someone will gaze down on us,
> And say: They made no fuss——
> For this was their finest shower.
> Yes, this was their finest shower!
> Thank God we're normal, normal, normal,
> Thank God we're normal,
> Yes, this is our finest shower!

EXIT ARCHIE.

NUMBER EIGHT

ARCHIE, FRANK, PHOEBE, JEAN, BILLY.

ARCHIE: She'd steal your knickers and sell 'em for dusters.

FRANK: Who?

ARCHIE: Mrs. Roberts, No. 7, Claypit Lane, always used to say that.

FRANK: Who are you talking about, you bloody right-wing old poup?

ARCHIE: I'm talking about that blonde bitch in the Cambridge, the one who's always upsetting your Grandad. And don't call me a right-wing old poup.

PHOEBE: I remember Mrs. Roberts. She was very nice to us.

ARCHIE: I may be an old poup, but I'm not a right-wing.

FRANK: That's strictly for cigar smokers like Grandad.
(*Dancing.*) "Oh, the end of me old cigar, cigar, the end of me old cigar, I turned 'em round and touched 'em

61

up with the end of me old cigar! The end of me old cigar, cigar, the end of me old cigar——"

ARCHIE: There was a chap at my school who managed to get himself into the Labour Government, and they always said he was left of centre. Then he went into the House of Lords, and they made him an honourable fishmonger. Well, that just about wraps up the Left of Centre, doesn't it?

FRANK: You know, you don't know what you're talking about.

BILLY: I used to have digs in Claypit Lane—ten shillings a week all-in.

PHOEBE: Frank, I thought you were going to sing.

ARCHIE: If you can dodge all the clichés dropping like bats from the ceiling, you might pick up something from me.

FRANK: Well, plenty of others have picked it up from you.

ARCHIE: Just you remember I'm your father.

FRANK: When did you ever remember it?

PHOEBE: Frank! Come on now, be a good boy.

ARCHIE: You want to be more like Jean——

FRANK: She's just not used to us any more. Are you, love? Are you all right?
Puts his arm round her.

JEAN: I'm all right.

FRANK: Are you really? Bet you'd forgotten what this was like, didn't you?

PHOEBE: Course she hadn't forgotten. She doesn't forget as easy as that, do you dear?

JEAN: No—I don't think so.

FRANK: (*to Phoebe*). You're feeling better?

PHOEBE: Yes, thank you, dear. Come over here and give me a kiss. (*He does so.*) He's a good boy to me, aren't you, dear? Even when I act a bit daft. We all act a bit daft sometimes, I suppose.

ARCHIE: Except Jean——

JEAN: Will you please stop trying to make me feel as if I were from another planet or something.

PHOEBE: Archie's just pulling your leg, aren't you Archie? I didn't have my Beecham's Pills yesterday. D'you know

62

my mother never had a doctor in her life—except when
we were born, of course. And all she ever took was two
pennorth of Beecham's, peroxide, and Dutch drops.

JEAN: Peroxide?

FRANK: She used to drink it like Guinness.

PHOEBE: Well, she lived to be ninety-three and never cost the
Government a penny. (*To Billy.*) All right?

BILLY: Yes, thank you, Phoebe.

PHOEBE: (*to Archie*). Put something in his glass, Archie. It's
nearly empty.

BILLY: I was just trying to remember the name of the woman.

PHOEBE: What woman?

BILLY: The one in Claypit Lane. She used to give us bacon
every morning for breakfast, and she'd melt cheese over
it. First time I'd ever had it.

PHOEBE: Don't like anything like that much. Here, did you—
pardon my interruption but I just remembered it—did
you see that picture of the Duchess of Porth's daughter
in the paper today?

FRANK: Should we?

PHOEBE: I wouldn't have seen it. I was only really reading about
Mick, of course, but I couldn't help noticing it. She
looked so fascinating. Did you see it, Archie?

ARCHIE: Oh yes. She was next to Captain Breech-Loading Gore.

PHOEBE: Didn't you think she looked magnificent?

ARCHIE: I thought she looked like Dad's barmaid in the
Cambridge.

FRANK: Yes—in drag.

PHOEBE: Frank!

ARCHIE: (*quickly*). Phoebe's very keen on the Duchess of Porth,
aren't you, love? She says she thinks she's natural.

PHOEBE: I suppose it's a bit silly, but I've always taken an
interest in her. Oh, ever since she was quite young. I
feel she must be very nice somehow. (*Pause.*) (*To
Archie.*) Is he all right? (*Nodding to Billy.*)

ARCHIE: He's all right. You're all right, aren't you?

BILLY: She always used to put cheese over the bacon.

ARCHIE: He's thinking about the landlady in Claypit Lane. You

63

know, that barmaid in the Cambridge reminds me of a bloke—(*To Jean*)—this'll interest you because it's Prime Ministers and Dogs—he was Irish, he did a trampoline act and they called him "Lady Rosie Bothways". Actually, he was a devout sort of a lad. He gave it all up later and went into Public Relations or something. Well, Rosie knew more dirty words than you'll hear in any place on any Saturday night. He could go on for ten minutes without pausing for breath, or repeating himself once. He was an artist. But to Rosie the most deadly four-letter word in the English—or any other— language, was Tory. He'd apply it to anything, pro- vided he thought it was really bad enough.

BILLY: I'll bet he was bloody Irish.

ARCHIE: I've just said so. Do try and listen.

PHOEBE: I thought Frank was going to sing.

ARCHIE: If you gave him a plate of badly cooked chips, he'd hold 'em up and say: "Who done these no-good, blank, blank, stinking, Tory chips?"

FRANK: You've told that story before.

ARCHIE: I'll bodge you in a minute.

FRANK: I'll bodge *you* in a minute. It's not even a very good story.

ARCHIE: When you learn to tell a story as well as I do, you'll be all right——

FRANK: I'll never look *old* enough, to tell your stories.

ARCHIE: I think you'd better sing, don't you?

FRANK: All right, all right, I will. I'll sing for Jean, because she hasn't heard me. I'm going to sing one of Billy's. It's British——

BILLY: What's that? What song?

FRANK: And very religious.

BILLY: What song's he singing?

FRANK: So there's something in it for you all.

He sings and dances.

When you've shouted Rule Britannia,
When you've sung God Save the Queen,
When you've finished killing Kruger with your
mouth,

Will you kindly drop a shilling in my little
    tambourine
For a gentleman in khaki ordered south.

He's an absent-minded beggar, and his weaknesses
    are great
But we informers take him as we find him,
For he's out on active service, wiping something
    off a slate
And he's left a lot of little things behind him.
Cook's son, duke's son, son of a belted earl——

Fifty thousand horse and foot ordered to Table
    Bay.
Each of 'em's doing his country's work——
And who's to look after the girl?
Pass the hat for your credit's sake, and pay,
    pay, pay!

BILLY: Pass the hat for your credit's sake, and pay, pay, pay.

ARCHIE: Not bad for an amateur.

BILLY: Last time I sang that was in a pub, some place in
Yorkshire. If you bought a pint of beer, you could get
a plateful of Yorkshire Pudding then, as much as you
could eat. All for tuppence.

ARCHIE: Come off it, Dad. Nobody ever gave away stuff like
that, not even when you remember.

BILLY: I tell you, you got a plate of Yorkshire Pudding——

ARCHIE: You're getting really old.

BILLY: As much as you could eat.

ARCHIE: Your mind's going, Dad. I should sit down.

BILLY: I *am* sitting down.

ARCHIE: Getting feeble.

PHOEBE: Archie—don't tease him.

BILLY: I'm not feeble! I'm not half as bloody feeble as you
are—thank God! (*Suddenly sees them smiling at him.*)
Thank God I'm not, that's all. You think you can have
it over me all right. Give me some of that!

FRANK: When there isn't a girl about you feel so lonely.

65

When there isn't a girl about you're on your only——

ARCHIE: Be quiet a minute, will you? I'm trying to think. Ah! yes. Yes. The girl I love is up in the lavatory, the girl I love is looking down on me.

PHOEBE: No don't do that, Archie. Don't sing it like that! (*To Jean and Frank.*) He always used to sing that song, didn't you? It was his favourite, I think.

JEAN: You sing it.

PHOEBE: Me—Oh I can't sing. I don't know even if I can remember the words.

FRANK: Go on, love, have a go.

PHOEBE: (*to Archie*). Shall I? (*He nods shortly.*) All right, then. *She sings:*

> Oh the boy I love he's up in the gallery
> The boy I love is looking down at me.
> Where is he?
> There is he,
> Waving of his handkerchee,
> Happy as the robin
> That sings on the tree.

JEAN: Thank you, Phoebe. Thank you.

PHOEBE: It sounded bloody awful, I expect.

BILLY: Well, I'm going to bed.

PHOEBE: Going already?

BILLY: (*going down to his room*). Yes, I only sat up to drink a toast to young Mick. I'm going to bed before you get those bloody Poles up here. Good night, everybody. *They all call out: "Good night."*

PHOEBE: I suppose I ought to go in a minute. I feel a bit tired. Still, I shan't go in to work tomorrow. Well, I shouldn't think they'll expect me to, would you?

JEAN: Of course not.

PHOEBE: Probably be too excited to sleep anyway. (*To Jean.*) Did I show you the letter I had from Clare?

JEAN: Who's Clare?

ARCHIE: (*to Phoebe*). I should go to bed, dear.

PHOEBE: Just a minute. I'm going to read her Clare's letter. Clare's my niece—that's the one in Toronto. I'd better read it to you, her writing's not very good. She's my brother John's daughter. They're all over there now, my brother John as well. They started off in the restaurant business four years ago with five hundred dollars—that's their little girl. (*Hands photograph to Jean.*) Now they've got a hotel in Toronto, and they're going to open another one.

ARCHIE: (*to Jean*). You don't have to look interested, dear. (*To Phoebe.*) She's not interested in all that horse manure about Canada.

PHOEBE: Of course she's interested. She doesn't mind listening, do you?

ARCHIE: Why doesn't Frank sing another song?

PHOEBE: I'm only trying to explain to her. They've opened one in Toronto, and now they're going to open another hotel in Ottawa. My brother John is managing the one in Toronto for them, but they want us to go out there, and for Archie to manage the hotel in Ottawa.

ARCHIE: What do I know about hotels? All I've lived in is digs.

PHOEBE: He gets cross if I mention it.

ARCHIE: For God's sake don't say I get cross if you mention it once more. You've mentioned it, haven't you? And I'm not cross! I just think it's a bloody pointless idea.

JEAN: When did they write this to you?

PHOEBE: About a fortnight now. Oh, she says we needn't make a decision for another month or two.

JEAN: What about the boys?

PHOEBE: They can come too if they want. I don't know about Mick, but Frank likes the idea, don't you?

JEAN: Do you, Frank?

FRANK: Look around you. Can you think of any good reason for staying in this cosy little corner of Europe? Don't kid yourself anyone's going to let you do anything, or try anything here, Jeannie. Because they're not. You haven't got a chance. Who are you—you're nobody. You're nobody, you've no money, and you're young. And when you end up it's pretty certain you'll still be nobody, you'll still have no money—the only difference is you'll be *old*! You'd better start thinking about number one, Jeannie, because nobody else is going to do it for you. Nobody else is going to do it for you because nobody believes in that stuff any more. Oh, they may say they do, and may take a few bob out of your pay packet every week and stick some stamps on your card to prove it, but don't believe it—nobody will give you a second look. They're all so busy, speeding down the middle of the road together, not giving a damn where they're going, as long as they're in the bloody middle! (*Chirpily, almost singing.*) *The rotten bastards!* "Oh when there isn't a girl about you feel so lonely. When there isn't a girl about you're on your only."

ARCHIE: Ssh, you'll wake up the Poles.

FRANK: Somebody should wake you up. "You're on your only!"

ARCHIE: You should go to bed.

FRANK: You and that blonde bitch in the Cambridge. You and her.

Like a monkey up a tree, I don't think! I'm going to bed.

He goes out singing, laying an arm on Archie's shoulder, and waving to the others.

ARCHIE: Good night, boy.

FRANK: (*singing*). "Rock of Ages cleft for me,
Let me hide myself in thee!"

Exit.

ARCHIE: Anyway you can't buy draught Bass in Toronto.

PHOEBE: Here, this is what she says: She talks about us coming out, and paying our fare, etc., and then the job in Ottawa. Experience isn't necessary, it's having your own people. She says: "We have a twenty-one inch T.V. set, a radio, etc. and now we have a 1956 Chevrolet Bel Air car complete with automatic shift and all the fancy gadgets everyone goes in for over here. I'm quite sure that you and Archie would settle down in no time, and everything would work out fine." (*She folds the letter up carefully*.) I thought you'd like to hear what she said.

68

JEAN: Yes, thank you.

PHOEBE: (*after a slight pause*). Are you staying up much longer, Archie?

ARCHIE: I'm just going.

PHOEBE: I think we're all tired. I can't take all this excitement any more. (*To Jean.*) Good night, dear. Forgive me being a bit silly, won't you?

JEAN: Forget it. Good night. I shan't wake you up.

PHOEBE: Good night, Archie.

ARCHIE: I'll come up and say good night.

PHOEBE: Thank you, dear. We'll have to find him somewhere to sleep, won't we?

ARCHIE: Mick? Oh, he can bed down here with me.

PHOEBE: Yes, I expect he'll be fagged out, poor kid. Oh, well, he won't be long now.
Exit.

ARCHIE: I went to Canada during the war.

JEAN: I remember.

ARCHIE: Couldn't get any draught Bass, not even in Toronto, and they seemed to reckon that was pretty English. (*Pause.*) Didn't seem very English to me. Can't get over you going to Trafalgar Square. Did you really care about all that?

JEAN: I thought I did at the time.

ARCHIE: Like draught Bass and women, eh? Did I ever tell you my nuns story? They just took one look at me—I can remember their white, unhealthy faces, and their little eyes—they took one look at me, and, together, at the same time, quite, quite spontaneously, they crossed themselves. They crossed themselves. And that was the biggest compliment I ever had paid to me in my whole life. Let's have some more of this, shall we?

JEAN: Sure.

ARCHIE: You were having trouble with Phoebe tonight.

JEAN: It was nothing much. She just seemed to suddenly turn on me.

ARCHIE: Your mother caught me in bed with Phoebe. (*Pause.*)

JEAN: I didn't know.

69

ARCHIE: I don't know what I really expected, but somehow I expected you to say something more than that.

JEAN: What do you expect me to do—hold a rally in Trafalgar Square?

ARCHIE: All my children think I'm a bum. I've never bothered to hide it, I suppose—that's the answer.

JEAN: Perhaps we should go to bed.

ARCHIE: No, stay up for a while. I think we're both in the mood. You'd just been born and your mother found poor old Phoebe and me together. Poor old Phoebe, she's never even enjoyed it very much. Your mother walked out, she walked out just like that. She was what you'd call a person of—a person of principle. She knew how people should behave, and there were no two ways about it. She never forgave me anyway.

JEAN: You didn't love her——

ARCHIE is drunk, and he sings and orchestrates his speech as only a drunken man can, almost objectively and fastidiously, like a conductor controlling his own sound.

ARCHIE: Yes, I loved her. I was in love with her, whatever that may mean. I don't know. Anyway, a few months later she was dead and that was that. She felt everything very deeply, your mother. Much more deeply than I did. Perhaps we could have worked it out between us. Did I ever tell you the most moving thing that I ever heard? It was when I was in Canada—I managed to slip over the border sometimes to some people I knew, and one night I heard some negress singing in a bar. *Now you're going to smile at this*, you're going to smile your educated English head off, because I suppose you've never sat lonely and half slewed in some bar among strangers a thousand miles from anything you think you understand. But if ever I saw any hope or strength in the human race, it was in the face of that old fat negress getting up to sing about Jesus or something like that. She was poor and lonely and oppressed like nobody you've ever known. Or me, for that matter. I never even liked that kind of music, but to see that

70

old black whore singing her heart out to the whole world, you knew somehow in your heart that it didn't matter how much you kick people, the real people, how much you despise them, if they can stand up and make a pure, just natural noise like that, there's nothing wrong with them, only with everybody else. I've never heard anything like that since. I've never heard it here. Oh, I've heard whispers of it on a Saturday night somewhere. Oh, he's heard it. Billy's heard it. He's heard them singing. Years ago, poor old gubbins. But you won't hear it anywhere now. I don't suppose we'll ever hear it again. There's nobody who can feel like that. I wish to God I could, I wish to God I could feel like that old black bitch with her fat cheeks, and sing. If I'd done one thing as good as that in my whole life, I'd have been all right. Better than all your getting on with the job without making a fuss and all that, or doing something constructive and all that, all your rallies in Trafalgar Square! I wish to God I were that old bag. I'd stand up and shake my great bosom up and down, and lift up my head and make the most beautiful fuss in the world. Dear God, I would. But I'll never do it. I don't give a damn about anything, not even women or draught Bass. Do you think that you're going to do it? Well, do you?

JEAN: I don't know. I just really don't know. I'll probably do exactly the same as you.

ARCHIE: Of course you will. Mind you, you'll make a better job of it. You're more clever, I think you really feel something too, in spite of all that Trafalgar Square stuff. You're what they call a sentimentalist. You carry all your responses about with you, instead of leaving them at home. While everyone else is sitting on their hands you're the Joe at the back cheering and making his hands hurt. But you'll have to sit on your hands like everyone else. Oh, you think I'm just a tatty old music hall actor who should be told the truth, like Old Billy, that people don't wear sovereign cases and patent leather

71

shoes any more. You know when you're up there
you think you love all those people around you out
there, but you don't. You don't love them, you're not
going to stand up and make a beautiful fuss. If you
learn it properly you'll get yourself a technique. You
can smile, darn you, smile, and look the friendliest
jolliest thing in the world, but you'll be just as dead
and smug and used up, and sitting on your hands just
like everybody else. You see this face, you see this face,
this face can split open with warmth and humanity. It
can sing, and tell the worst, unfunniest stories in the
world to a great mob of dead, drab erks and it doesn't
matter, it doesn't matter. It doesn't matter because—
look at my eyes. I'm dead behind these eyes. I'm dead,
just like the whole inert, shoddy lot out there. It
doesn't matter because I don't feel a thing, and neither
do they. We're just as dead as each other. Tell me, tell
me something. I want you to tell me something. What
would you say to a man of my age marrying a girl of—
oh about your age? Don't be shocked. I told you—I
don't feel a thing.

JEAN: You couldn't! You couldn't do a thing like that!

ARCHIE: You've been away from your old Dad a bit too long.
We've never seen much of each other, have we? Well,
never mind.

JEAN: You're not serious! You couldn't do that to Phoebe—
not a divorce.

ARCHIE: Children! (*Laughs.*) Children! They're like the bloody
music hall. Don't worry about your old man—he's still
a bit worried about young Mick. At least, I suppose he
is. I told you, nothing really touches me. As the man
said, I've paid me one and saxpence—I defy yez to
entertain me! Let anyone get up there and give a performance, let them get up, I don't care how good it is.
Old Archie, dead behind the eyes, is sitting on his
hands, he lost his responses on the way. You wouldn't
think I was sexy to look at me, would you? You
wouldn't think I was sexy to look at me, would you?

Well, I 'ave a go, lady. I 'ave a go, don't I? I do. I 'ave a go. That barmaid in the Cambridge. That barmaid who upset poor old Billy in the Cambridge—I had her! When he wasn't looking. . . .

Enter Phoebe.

PHOEBE: I thought you'd got somebody here. They called up from downstairs. There's a policeman at the door for you, Archie.

ARCHIE: It's the income-tax man. It's the income-tax man. Tell him I've been expecting him. I've been expecting him for twenty years.

PHOEBE: (*to Jean*). I thought he had someone in here. What do you think he wants?

ARCHIE: Just me and my daughter Jean. Me and my daughter Jean—by my first love. Why don't you go back to London? Say, aren't you glad you're normal? I've always been a seven day a week man myself, haven't I, Phoebe? A seven day a week man. I always needed a jump at the end of the day—and at the beginning too usually. Just like a piece of bacon on the slab. Well, it's everybody's problem. Unless you're like Mick and have got no problem. Well, he had a problem, but now he's on his way. Yes, that's a boy without problems. I'm a seven day a week man myself, twice a day. Poor old Phoebe, don't look so scared, love. Either they're doing it, and they're not enjoying it. Or else they're not doing it and they aren't enjoying it. Don't look so scared, love. Archie's drunk again. It's only the income tax man!

PHOEBE: Frank's down there——

FRANK: (*in*). The bastards! *The rotten bastards!* They've killed him! They've killed Mick! Those bloody wogs—they've murdered him. Oh, the rotten bastards!

ARCHIE: (*slowly singing a blues*). Oh, lord, I don't care where they bury my body, no I don't care where they bury my body, 'cos my soul's going to live with God!

CURTAIN

END OF ACT TWO

Blues. Spot on FRANK at piano.

FRANK: Bring back his body, and bury it in England.
Bring back his body, and bury it here.
Bring back his body, in an aeroplane.
But don't ever talk to me.
Those playing fields of Eton
Have really got us beaten.
But ain't no use agrievin'
'Cos it's Britain we believe in.
So bring back his body, and bury it here.
Bring back his body in an aeroplane——
But just don't ever talk to me.

FADE

NUMBER TEN

BILLY, PHOEBE, JEAN, FRANK, ARCHIE. BILLY and
PHOEBE are dressed in black. The others wear black
arm bands.

JEAN: Well, that's that. (*Picks up some newspapers.*) Can anyone tell me what the whole thing added up to? (*Pause.*)

ARCHIE: My aunt always used to say the same thing, "Well,
they gave him a good send off." Always said it without
fail. (*To Billy.*) Didn't she?

BILLY: Poor old Rosie.

ARCHIE: I used to wonder what would happen if she didn't say
it.

BILLY: Old Rosie and me used to have some good times
together. Used to go out a lot. Before we were both
married.

JEAN: Well, I suppose it gives somebody a kick. Are you all
right, Phoebe?

PHOEBE: I'm all right, dear. A bit tired.

BILLY: What a place London was then for having a good time. Best place in the world for a laugh. People were always ready to laugh, to give you a welcome. Best audience in the world.

Crosses L.C. Gets chair and sits above table.

ARCHIE: I was in a little village in Donegal once. On the Irish fit-ups. (*To Billy.*) You remember. The morning we arrived there, a man came up to me and said: "Oh, we're great students of the drama here. Great students of the drama. Our dramatic critics can lick anyone— anyone!" Turned out he was the local blacksmith. He said, he said: "If you get past an audience here, you'll get past any audience in the world." It was true too. Think I got a black eye.

BILLY: Some places, they just sit back and stare at you. They just—sit. But, London, that was the place. Old Rosie— she was a beautiful woman. I'm glad she's not here now.

JEAN: (*grabbing at newspapers*). How can you compete against this stuff?

FRANK: You can't.

JEAN: Why didn't somebody get a picture of you stoking your boilers?

ARCHIE: I don't think Mick would have taken it too seriously.

FRANK: Everybody's tired.

JEAN: Everybody's tired all right. Everybody's tired, everybody's standing about, loitering without any intent whatsoever, waiting to be picked up by whatever they may allow to happen to us next.

ARCHIE: Jesus, don't start getting emotional——

JEAN: I don't expect you to.

ARCHIE: That's right.

JEAN: But Frank's different—at least, I hope he is. You don't have to be afraid, Frank. You needn't worry about being emotional, like my talented fiancé. You won't die of it. You may think you can, but you won't.

ARCHIE: Old Mick was a bit like Graham actually. He seemed to know what he wanted, and where he was going.

75

JEAN: Did he now, that's interesting——

ARCHIE: I remember he was having an affair with a girl called Sylvia. He was about sixteen at the time.

JEAN: What's the matter with you, Archie?

FRANK: Why don't you leave him alone?

ARCHIE: That's right, why don't you leave your old man alone?

JEAN: Oh, you've been left alone all right!

ARCHIE: Shall I tell you—all my life I've been searching for something. I've been searching for a draught Bass you can drink all the evening without running off every ten minutes, that you can get drunk on without feeling sick, and all for fourpence. Now, the man who could offer me all of that would really get my vote. He really would. Oh, well, I could always make a woman better than I could make a point.

JEAN: You know, Archie, you're a bit of a bastard.

PHOEBE: Jean——

JEAN: You really are—you're a bastard on wheels!

ARCHIE: Because I don't care about anything except draught Bass? Listen, kiddie, you're going to find out that in the end nobody really gives a damn about anything except some little animal something. And for me that little animal something is draught Bass. Now why can't you stop attacking everyone?

JEAN: I can't.

ARCHIE: What do you think you are—a dose of salts?

JEAN: I owe it to myself.

ARCHIE: Well, I never really believed in all that inner cleanliness anyway. Did I leave a bottle of beer in here last night?

PHOEBE: I don't think so, dear.

ARCHIE: If you're not careful, Jean, people will start putting labels on you pretty soon. And then you'll just be nobody. You'll be nobody like the rest of us.

PHOEBE: Frank'll get you some. There's some left in the kitchen. Would you mind, dear?

FRANK: Sure. (*Rises. Crosses L. of chair.*)

JEAN: We can't all spend our time nailing our suitcases to the floor, and shin out of the window.

ARCHIE: Scarper the letty.

JEAN: You're like everybody else, but you're worse—you think you can cover yourself by simply not bothering. (*Newspapers.*) You think if you don't bother you can't be humiliated, so you just roar your life out in four-letter words and just hope that somehow the perks will turn up.

FRANK: Leave him alone, he's just as upset as you are! So shut up.

JEAN: I'll give you the Archie Rice story. All right. You want the credit titles first?

ARCHIE: I didn't like the clergyman, anyway. I really hated him. He was as chloe as all get out. Did you notice?

JEAN: You don't fool me. You couldn't fool pussy!

ARCHIE: Go on—insult me, I don't mind. One thing I've discovered a long time ago. Most people never know when they're being insulted. And a whole lot of people make a whole lot of money out of that principle. I'm as dim as a bucket really. You know. I'm no better than the rest of them.

JEAN: Oh now, don't start being humble——

ARCHIE: I *am* humble! I am very humble, in fact. I still have a little dried pea of humility rattling around inside me. I don't think *you* have.

JEAN: And that's just about all.

FRANK: What's the matter with her?

ARCHIE: Don't ask me, son. Don't ask me. I've never solved a problem in my life.

JEAN: You haven't got the nous. You've been too busy hating all those feckless moochers out there in the great darkness, haven't you? You've been really smart. (*To Frank.*) I'd like you to know the truth about your father.

FRANK: Listen, Jean, Mick's just been buried. He's buried and nobody wants to start talking about it, or having rows.

JEAN: What do you want, two minutes silence? Not only is your father generous, understanding and sympathetic— he doesn't give a damn about anyone. He's two pen-north of nothing.

77

ARCHIE: Yes, I should say that sums me up pretty well.

JEAN: You don't need to look at me! I've lost a brother too. Why do people like us sit here, and just lap it all up, why do boys die, or stoke boilers, why do we pick up these things, what are we hoping to get out of it, what's it all in aid of—is it really just for the sake of a gloved hand waving at you from a golden coach?

PHOEBE: I think I'll go and lie down. (*To Jean.*) He's always been good to me.

FRANK: Shall I bring you up an aspirin?

JEAN: Nobody listens to anyone.

PHOEBE: Thank you, dear. If you wouldn't mind. (*To Jean, simply.*) He's always been good to me. Whatever he may have done. Always.
Exit.

FRANK: I'll get you that beer.

BILLY: Always had a decanter on the sideboard at home. I've got the key here.

JEAN: (*to Archie*). You can't do it to her, I won't let you.

BILLY: Yes, here it is.

ARCHIE: He wants to know if I've renewed the ticket. It's all right—I've got another three months on it.

BILLY: Eh? (*To Jean.*) There.

JEAN: What's this?

BILLY: What's the matter—you want your bloody ears syringed?

FRANK: You want some beer, Grandad?

BILLY: Nobody listens to a bloody word you're saying.

FRANK: I said do you want some beer?

BILLY: That's the trouble nowadays. Everybody's too busy answering back and taking liberties. 'Stead of getting on with it and doing as they're told. No, I'm going to bed. I've got to be out early tomorrow. (*To Archie.*) What time did you say?

ARCHIE: About nine.

FRANK: Where are you going?

BILLY: Your father and I have got some business together. Seemed funny all those people taking off their hats to young Mick today.

FRANK: Most of 'em weren't wearing hats anyway.

BILLY: When I was younger, every man—and every man wore a hat in those days, didn't matter if he was a lord or a butcher—every man used to take his hat off when he passed the Cenotaph. Even in the bus. Nowadays I've watched people just go past it, not even a look. If you took the flags off of it I expect they'd sit down and eat their sandwiches on it.

ARCHIE: I was just thinking of young Mick and Sylvia. She was a nice, attractive little kid. I wonder what she's doing now. I wonder if she's read about him in the papers. Being a national hero and getting killed. I shouldn't think she'd have forgotten him already, would you?

FRANK: I shouldn't think so. Can I have some of your beer?

ARCHIE: Help yourself. I remember being worried about Sylvia. I couldn't get it out of young Mick, and I had an idea she was under-age. It worried me just a bit. I tried to tackle him about it, but he always thought I was a bit of a chump, he did, you know. Oh, I didn't mind. I rather liked it. (*To Jean.*) He didn't really take me seriously. I hummed and hah'ed, and finally I said: "Well, look boy, I obviously don't have to tell you to take precautions." He just grinned like the clappers, and I suddenly felt like some weird old clergyman. So I just said to him: "Well, anyway, you do know what the age of consent is, don't you?" And he sat there with that great awful grin on his face, and said: "Sixteen".

JEAN: Where are you taking Billy tomorrow?

ARCHIE: I think I'll have to go back to Brighton, and become a Beachcomber.

FRANK: (*to Jean*). Got any aspirins on you? There don't seem to be any.

ARCHIE: Edlins—that was the place. All over Brighton.

JEAN: (*giving Frank aspirins*). Don't you know what he's trying to do?

ARCHIE: You could get nicely oiled on their draught cider for a few pence.

FRANK: Why don't you leave them alone?

79

ARCHIE: Haven't had it for years. How much was it?

JEAN: He thinks he's going to divorce her. He thinks he's going to divorce Phoebe. I've seen her—this girl he wants to marry. He's crazy. That's what he is. What's going to happen to her? (*She nods upstairs.*)

FRANK: What's going to happen to any of us. Listen, Jean, love—darling heart, you are not going to change anybody——

JEAN: Have you seen her? I caught them together yesterday. In the Rockliffe. I've seen her all right. She's a professional virgin.

ARCHIE: I wonder what it's like now. (*To Billy.*) How much did it use to be?

FRANK: I'd better take these (*aspirins*) up to her.

BILLY: What?

ARCHIE: Draught cider, you old gubbins.

BILLY: How the bloody hell should I know? I've never drunk the stuff.

ARCHIE: Yes, it's a bit acid, I suppose.

BILLY: 'Bout a penny, I should say. Penny a pint.

ARCHIE: Be about a bob now, I 'spect. (*Slight pause.*) Might as well drink beer.

JEAN: (*to Archie*). She's pretty, she's spoilt, she's vain, and she's stupid. And her parents are probably stupid. They must be, they must be stupid to produce her—Miss Nothing of 1957.

ARCHIE: That's right.

JEAN: How old is she?

ARCHIE: Twenty.

JEAN: Twenty. They're so stupid, I suppose, they'll even let her marry you?

ARCHIE: You know, I think I've only slept with one passionate woman. What I'd call really passionate. And she was happily married. Her name was Ivy.

JEAN: I suppose you think you'll get them to put up some money for you too?

ARCHIE: That was the idea.

JEAN: You're going to get her to put a ring through your nose, and tell yourself you won't feel it, because

80

nothing matters to you any more, and nobody else does either. You think because you can't get her, nobody else can! What about Phoebe?

ARCHIE: Ivy Williams, that's her name. Mrs. Ivy Williams. Mrs. Ivy Williams.

BILLY: Well, I'm off. Who're we seeing: Rubens?

ARCHIE: Klein.

BILLY: Charlie Klein. Old Charlie Klein. I was in the first show he ever put on the road, you know that?

ARCHIE: Twelve thirty.

BILLY: He was younger than Jeannie here. I made him a member of the National Sporting Club. It was me who put him up.

ARCHIE: He's a tough bastard.

BILLY: Oh, Charlie should be all right. It was me made him sign up Eddie Drummer. Good artist, Eddie. Been earning a thousand a week for twenty-five years, and just the same. He's a good boy. He's a sort of in-between. He wasn't one of us real old timers, and he wasn't one of these new five-minute wonders with a micro-phone. They've got no real personality now. He always had style, Eddie, and never any real suggestion of offence in anything he did. We all had our own style, our own songs—and we were all English. What's more, we spoke English. It was different. We all knew what the rules were. We knew what the rules were, and even if we spent half our time making people laugh at 'em we never seriously suggested that anyone should break them. A real pro is a real man, all he needs is an old backcloth behind him and he can hold them on his own for half an hour. He's like the general run of people, only he's a lot more like them than they are themselves, if you understand me. Well, Eddie's still up there all right. He's still up there. (*To Jean*.) I always used to say to him, we all used to say: "Eddie—always be good to the people on the way up, because you may meet them on the way down." Old Eddie. One of the really great ones, I should say he is. I should say he's pro-

bably the last. Yes, I should say he's probably the last.
Exit.

JEAN: What are you doing, what are you going to do to him?
You're not going to put him back into the business?

ARCHIE: Rubens and Klein twelve-thirty tomorrow morning——

JEAN: You're going to kill that old man just to save that no-
good, washed-up tatty show of yours——

ARCHIE: It isn't just to save that no-good, tatty show of mine.
It's to save your no-good tatty Dad from going to jail.
People may not come to see Archie but they may still
remember Billy Rice. It's worth a try anyway.

JEAN: Are you going to destroy that too? He's the only one of
us who has any dignity or respect for himself, he's the
only one of us who has anything at all, and you're going
to murder him, you're going to take him down to—who
is it—Rubens and Klein tomorrow morning at twelve-
thirty, and you're going to let Mr. Rubens and Mr.
Klein sign his death certificate. What are you letting
yourself in for now, how on earth did you ever get him
to do such a thing? What's happened to him? What's
happened to his sense of self preservation?

ARCHIE: He feels he owes it to me.

JEAN: Owes it to you! Owes it to you! Billy doesn't owe you
or anyone anything.

ARCHIE: You see, before you got busy lecturing me about inner
cleanliness, Billy went and did something. He went and
saw my little girl friend's parents, you know, the professional virgin you saw in the Rockliffe. He went and
told them I was a married man with three grown-up
children. Three acknowledged—anyway, but I don't
suppose old Billy needed to mention the rest of them.

JEAN: He scotched it!

ARCHIE: Oh, yes—completely. You see, I hadn't told them about
—about Phoebe, and all of you.

JEAN: No, I suppose you wouldn't.

ARCHIE: So you see you weren't wrong, Jeannie, love. Not about
Phoebe anyway—old Archie isn't going to get his oats
after all.

NUMBER ELEVEN

ARCHIE: Ladies and Gentlemen, Billy Rice will not appear tonight.
Billy Rice will not appear again. I wish I could sing a song
for him—in his place. A farewell. But, unfortunately, I
can't. Nobody can. None of us, any way.
Exit.
Front Gauze. Funeral cortège with ARCHIE, PHOEBE,
JEAN, FRANK, GRAHAM and BROTHER BILL. They
gather round a coffin C. stage, draping over it a Union
Jack, Billy's hat, cane, and gloves. In the background,
snatches of old songs, wisps of tunes, the stumble of a
banjo. Fade to——

NUMBER TWELVE

Down L. A lime drenches ARCHIE and BROTHER BILL.
Down R. lime on JEAN and GRAHAM DODD. BROTHER BILL
looks like a highly successful and distinguished lawyer,
and he is. GRAHAM DODD may well be like him in thirty
years, provided he is successful. There are plenty of
these around—well dressed, assured, well educated,
their emotional and imaginative capacity so limited it is
practically negligible. They have an all-defying inability
to associate themselves with anyone in circumstances
even slightly dissimilar to their own. GRAHAM DODD
doesn't need much description. If you can't recognize
him, it's for one reason only. These two duologues are
independent, but run together.

GRAHAM: Quite honestly, Jean, I don't mean to be rude. I mean,
well it is rude to come out and say it, but I can't see
what you can possibly have in common with any of
them.

JEAN: You can't——

GRAHAM: Well, they're your family and all that, but after all, there does come a point, there does come a point in things——

ARCHIE: He was such a sweet old man. He really was. D'you know who said that? Charlie Klein. Charlie Klein said old Billy was the nicest old man in the business.

GRAHAM: —you just don't have any more responsibility to people.

ARCHIE: And still a first-class performer, Archie. Still a first-class performer!

GRAHAM: —it's your background and you were brought up in it, but there are better, more worthwhile things in life.

ARCHIE: He was one of the great, one of the really great.

JEAN: I'm sorry, Graham. I'm staying with Phoebe. I told you I'd really made up my mind before I left. I can't marry you, and I don't want to any more. Anyway, I've got to stay here. Now that Billy's dead Phoebe needs someone with her. Frank's off to Canada in a couple of weeks——

ARCHIE: Jean thinks I killed him.

BROTHER BILL: You didn't kill him, Archie. You don't kill people that easily. I don't think so.

JEAN: We live differently. You and I don't even draw breath in the same way.

BROTHER BILL: Look, Archie. This is the last time for you. It's got to be Canada. You and Frank and Phoebe can all go out together. Your passages are all booked. I've got them in my pocket here. There're yours. You can go out and start a new life, the three of you.

GRAHAM: Oh, this is just rubbish. You're no different from me. You were in love with me, you said so. We enjoyed ourselves together. We could make a good thing of it. I've got quite a decent career lined up. We would have everything we want. Come back with me, Jean.

ARCHIE: You can't get draught Bass in Toronto. I've tried it.

JEAN: Have you ever got on a railway train here, got on a train from Birmingham to West Hartlepool? Or gone from Manchester to Warrington or Widnes. And you get out, you go down the street, and on one side maybe is a chemical works, and on the other side is the railway

84

goods yard. Some kids are playing in the street, and you walk up to some woman standing on her doorstep. It isn't a doorstep really because you can walk straight from the street into her front room. What can you say to her? What real piece of information, what message can you give to her? Do you say: "Madam, d'you know that Jesus died on the Cross for you?"

BROTHER BILL: Those tickets are yours, Archie. Now take them. I'll pay up all your debts, I'll settle everything, I'll see that nothing happens.

JEAN: And then the woman, she looks back at you, and she says: "Oh, yes, I heard all about that."

ARCHIE: What happens if I don't go?

BROTHER BILL: I'm not doing anything for you to stay here, Archie. Not any more. You'll just have to take the consequences I'm afraid. It's Canada or jail.

ARCHIE: You know, I've always thought I should go to jail. I should think it must be quite interesting. Sure to meet someone I know. D'you know what my landlady in Fulham used to say about you? She used to say: "He looks like a governor's man." Always said it—without fail.

GRAHAM: We're all in it for what we can get out of it. Isn't that what your father was supposed to say?

ARCHIE: You can never get anything at this Labour Exchange anyway. They must have more bums in this place than in any other town in England. Oh, well, thanks anyway, just two more performances. It's a pity though—I should have liked to notch up twenty-one against the income-tax man. I'll never make my twenty-first now. It would have been fun to get the key of the door, somehow.

JEAN: Here we are, we're alone in the universe, there's no God, it just seems that it all began by something as simple as sunlight striking on a piece of rock. And here we are. We've only got ourselves. Somehow, we've just got to make a go of it. *We've only ourselves.*

BROTHER BILL: I'm sorry, Archie, but I've given up trying to understand.

FADE.

85

Rock-n-Roll. Nude tableau, behind first act gauze.
Britannia. Then; the Archie Rice music, the one and
only, interrupting the programme. The stage blacks out.
A lime picks out the prompt corner, and ARCHIE makes
his entrance. He sings a few bars of "We're all out for
good old Number One".

ARCHIE: We're all out for good old Number One
        Number One's the only one for me.
        Good old England, you're my cup of tea,
        But I don't want no drab equality.
        Don't let your feelings roam,
        But remember that charity begins at home.
        What we've got left back
        We'll keep—and blow you, Jack.
        Number One's the only one for me.
           —God bless you,
        Number One's the only one for me.

I've just come to tell you about the wife. She's gone
back to her husband. She has, straight. Don't clap too
hard, we're all in a very old building. Yes, very old.
Old. What about *that*? What about *her*, eh—Madam
with the helmet on? I reckon she's sagging a bit, if you
ask me. She needs some beef putting into her—the
roast beef of old England. No, nobody's asking me,
never mind. Nice couple of fried eggs, anyway. She's
a nice girl, though—a nice girl. Going steady with
Charlie here—isn't she, Charlie? (*To the conductor.*)
She met him in a revolving door, and they've been
going around together ever since. I'm doing me nut,
you know that, don't you? I'm doing me nut up here.
Nudes, that's what they call them, lady, nudes. Blimey,
she's got more clothes on than I have. It's a lot of
madam, that's all it is. A lot of madam. Oh, I put a
line in there. Never mind, it doesn't matter. I've made

a few tumbles in my time. I have, honest. You wouldn't
think I was sexy to look at me, would you? No,
honestly, you wouldn't, would you, lady. I always
reckon you feel stronger after it? (*Sings.*) "Say, your
jelly-roll is fine, but it don't compare with mine!"
There's a bloke at the side here with a hook, you know
that, don't you? He is, he's standing there. I can see
him. Must be the income-tax man. Life's funny though,
isn't it? It is—life's funny. It's like sucking a sweet
with the wrapper on. Oh, well, we're all in the fertilizer
business now, I suppose. Well, I'd rather have a glass of
beer any day—I would. You don't believe me, but I
would. You think I'm gone, don't you? Go on, say it,
you think I'm gone. You think I'm gone, don't you?
Well, I am. What's the matter, you feeling cold up
there? Before I do go, ladies and gentlemen, I should
just like to tell you a little story, a little story. This
story is about a man, just a little, ordinary man, like
you and me, and one day he woke up and found himself in paradise. Well, he looks up, you see, and he sees
a feller standing next to him. It turns out that this feller
is a saint or something. Anyway, he's on the welcoming
committee. And the feller says to him—the Saint—says
to him: "Well," he says, "you're now in paradise." "Am
I?" he says. "You are," says the Saint. "What's more,
you have earned yourself eternal happiness." "Have I?"
he says. "You most certainly have," says the Saint.
"Oh, you're well away," he says. "Can't you hear the
multitudes? Why, everyone is singing, everyone is joy-
ful. What do you say, my son?" So the little man took
a look around him at all the multitudes of the earth,
spread out against the universe. So he says to the Saint:
"Well, can I get up where you're standing, and take a
proper look?" So the Saint says: "Of course you can,
my son" and makes way for him. And the little man
stood up where the Saint was and gazed up at the sight
around him. At all the Hosts of Heaven, and all the rest
of it. "All the wonder and the joy of eternity is round

about you," said the Saint. "You mean, this is all
eternity and I'm in Paradise?" "That is so, my son.
Well, what have you to say?" So the little man looks
around again for a bit, and the Saint says: "Well, my
son?" "Well," he says, "I've often wondered what I'd
say if this ever happened to me. I couldn't think somehow." And the Saint smiled at him kindly and says
again: "And what *do* you say, my son?" "Only one
thing I can say," says the little man. And he said it!
Well, the Saint looked as if he had been struck across
the face by some great hand. The Hosts stopped singing and all the Angels hid their faces, and for a tiny
splash in eternity there was no sound at all in Paradise.
The Saint couldn't speak for a while, and then he threw
his arms round the little man, and kissed him. And he
said: "I love you, my son. With all my soul, I shall love
you always. I have been waiting to hear that word ever
since I came here." He's there with his little hook, I can
see him. Oh, well, I have a go, don't I? I 'ave a go.
The cloth goes up, revealing a dark bare stage. The
music starts up softly, and ARCHIE RICE stands on the
stage in a little round world of light, and swaggers
gently into his song:

> Why should I care
> Why should I let it touch me,
> Why shouldn't I sit down and cry
> To let it pass over me?

He begins to falter a little.

> Why should——
> Why should I let it get me——
> What's the use of despair?

*He stops and stares ahead of him. The music goes on, then
he picks up.*

> If they see that you're blue
> They'll look down on you.

He stares up, then goes on.

> So why oh why should I bother to care?

PHOEBE appears L. holding a raincoat and hat.

ARCHIE: Why should I care,
                   Why should I let it touch me,
                   Why shouldn't I?——

He stops, the music goes on, as he walks over to PHOEBE, who helps him on with his coat, and gives him his hat. He hesitates, comes back down to the floats.

You've been a good audience. Very good. A very *good* audience. Let me know where you're working tomorrow night—and I'll come and see *YOU*.

He walks upstage with PHOEBE. The spotlight is hitting the apron, where ARCHIE has been standing. The orchestra goes on playing: "Why should I care"; suddenly, the little world of light snaps out, the stage is bare and dark. ARCHIE RICE has gone. There is only the music.

CURTAIN

THE END

89